TESTIMONIALS

Kerrie's book impressively shows how the magic of interpersonal psychology can happen. Using many of her own examples, she illustrates what is crucial, especially in stormy times: personal contact with our fellow human beings. Her companions also prove with small episodes of their own how exciting and enriching it can be to talk to strangers. This book is an encouraging plea for more interpersonal contact, helpfulness and social competence.

Dr. Frank Hagenow, Psychologist,
Certified Speaking Professional

How To Talk To Strangers provides an enlightening perspective on the positive impact we can have on others if we simply dare to connect with them, even with relatively small gestures of kindness such as by showing empathy or perhaps offering some guidance along the way. As shown through the wonderful stories Kerrie offers in this book, such acts of kindness can set off ripple effects of confidence building, helping others get out of low-points of their lives and to fulfill their dreams. Conversely, this book serves as a good reminder about the magnitude of the untapped potential that likely passes us by on the street on a daily basis if we don't reach out and simply talk to strangers.

Niklas Myhr, PhD, CSP,
The Social Media Professor

There are no coincidences, only missed opportunities to connect through lack of awareness and judgement. The shared wisdom from Kerrie and the stories within these pages teaches that we all make a difference to each other. This book made me reflect upon the fact that all of my patients when I meet them are strangers. In a short amount of time I have to connect with them so that they trust me with their life. I also considered the impact each of those strangers have upon me and what an incredible blessing not only am I to them but each patient is to me.

Dr Emila Dauway,
Oncologist, Surgeon, author of Live Fearlessly

Kerrie Phipps cares. And she understands deeply that that's the key to connection. Kerrie makes it so easy for us to implement this truth from my fellow TEDx Speaker, Brené Brown: 'Connection is why we're here. It's what brings meaning and purpose to our lives.' That's precisely what Kerrie brings to everything she does. And you'll feel it jumping out at you from every page, every sentence of this great book.

Paul Dunn,
Co Founder, B1G1

Wonderfully uplifting, empowering and revelatory. I used to fear it, but now I am actually excited about talking to strangers and creating positive ripple effects.

Steve Pipe,
author of Our Time To Rise

I love the stories shared in this book about the power of connection. Regardless of our age, race, background, or economic status, we share one thing in common - we desire authentic connection. This book shows why it is important to learn to connect with other people and how we can do that.

Sha Nacino,
Keynote Speaker, Founder, World Gratitude Summit™

Previously, I was very introverted. Since I read Kerrie's book DO Talk To Strangers and mastered the Asking Model I am connecting with strangers confidently. The purpose of life is to help, to guide, to lead, to build, to serve, and to show compassion, love and the will to help others whom you know and don't know at all. How to Talk to Strangers is compiled with many inspiring stories and will help you raise your level of Awareness and have a glimpse of wonderful realities.

Rajiv Nagar,
Entrepreneur and Speaker

A glorious collection of inspiring stories, from inspiring people, reminding us what's really important in life - human connection! It comes in so many forms, it happens everywhere, and it's a beautiful part of the journey of life, if we keep our eyes open to the gift of connection when it shows up.

Andrea T Edwards,
CSP, author of Uncommon Courage

Moments in people's lives are shared so beautifully in this book. I know as you read you will be touched, inspired and have a greater awareness that our everyday lives can change the trajectory of others.

Allyson Gray,
Professional Certified Coach, Educator

Through her books, Kerrie brings out a unique approach to her readers, that opens up a new world of confidence and delivers the impact of talking to strangers. Today, I think Kerrie is doing what she is doing purely because she tunes into the energy that she wants to spread. Kerrie is specialised and mastered, and teaches people to get out of their mobile phones and connect. I'm pumped about How to Talk to Strangers as these stories from across the world will inspire more people to talk to strangers and make a positive difference.

Dr. K.K.Ramachandran,
Director, GRD College, Coimbatore, India

Kerrie Phipps does it again, following on from her Do Talk to Strangers Book, she's now compiled an amazing collection of stories of everyday people and their wonderful adventures plus the lessons they learned, whilst talking to other people, sometimes total strangers. She often quotes on stage that "You make a bigger difference than you know" and those words reverberate so well inside this book. Time and again, we read examples of how total strangers have had a profound influence on the contributors to this book. Compelling, feel good and educational reading, well done to Kerrie and her co-authors.

Lindsay Adams OAM
Author of The DNA of Business Relationships

How To Talk To Strangers
to Decrease Anxiety, Build Confidence and Make a Bigger Difference in the World.

By Kerrie Phipps

KERRIE
PHIPPS
Connect with Confidence

Published by Create the Life Club Pty Ltd

Cover design Nathan Shooter, Brandhood Media
Internal design and Layout Amit Dey

Quotes are attributed within the book
Copyright © 2021 Kerrie Phipps
First Edition: 2021 (Paperback, eBook)

National Library of Australia Cataloguing-in-Publication entry

Creator: Phipps, Kerrie Louise, author.
Title: How To Talk To Strangers
to Decrease Anxiety, Build Confidence and Make a Bigger Difference in the World.
ISBN: 978-0-9941573-4-8 (paperback)
ISBN: 978-0-9941573-5-5 (eBook)
Subjects: Interpersonal Relations. Self-Help Techniques.

HOW TO Talk TO
Strangers

HOW TO Talk TO
Strangers

TO DECREASE ANXIETY, BUILD CONFIDENCE AND MAKE A BIGGER DIFFERENCE IN THE WORLD.

KERRIE PHIPPS

with

Conor O'Malley • Katie Swanson • Simon Jacobs • Unami Magwenzi
Serene Seng • Anupama Singal • Anna Sheppard • Patrick Galvin
Kaley Chu • Ganesh Somwanshi • Julie Woods • Lyndon Phipps
Cathy Johnson • Masami Sato • Nathan Shooter

Every day
people are talked down from the ledge,
every day people are lifted, by words,
love and encouragement,
by the smiles of people
like you.

These moments can be
the reason people stay,
when all they want to do is leave,
the reason they go on,
when all they want to do is quit.

**Thank you for being someone's
good news story.**

TABLE OF CONTENTS

FOREWORD

Masami Sato

I'm an introvert.

And I definitely wouldn't be the best person to talk about 'talking to strangers'.

Years ago I was a very quiet, socially-awkward and timid little girl in Japan who had no idea what existed outside my own small community. I used to think that speaking to people I didn't know meant potentially offending them, being judged or hurting their feelings. So, I mostly lived inside my own mind - imagining a world where we were all free.

And then at 20-years of age, I decided to travel. It transformed my world. And it was again transformed by years of being in business working with people from all parts of the world.

Today, I am still the person who can be intimidated by the idea of talking to strangers. At networking events, I often experience this urge to hide in the bathroom - seriously! - rather than actively mingling with strangers.

So, let me admit it. I had no idea at first why Kerrie asked me to contribute to this book, to introduce this very idea to a wider audience. And thanks to Kerrie's persistence, I eventually realised that we fully agreed on a very core idea, 'it's about **connecting** with people that really matters'.

I discovered that I love connecting with others. I love discovering the unique qualities people bring to our world. And connecting with those strangers changed my world. I truly love the fact we can make extraordinary things happen together when we connect.

Over the last decade, working with Kerrie and others like her who've joined us in B1G1: Business for Good, we've created millions of smiles in the world - special impacts that transform lives and communities.

Now, more and more disadvantaged children are attending school, women are receiving support to start their own businesses, trees are being planted in native forests and in communities, food waste is collected and re-distributed to those who are in need of help and beaches are cleared of plastic trash … all because of the connections and bonds we formed with strangers.

You'll get to explore that very simple idea of 'kindness at work' in this book too.

I invite you to ponder on the power of human connection with me and with us - no matter whether you think you are an extrovert or an introvert.

Surprisingly, it starts with just one conversation, one smile, one interaction. That is all it takes - a look, a smile and a conversation. It's powerful.

And it really can change our world.

Masami Sato
Founder of B1G1, a global giving movement

INTRODUCTION

Unami Magwenzi

When Kerrie asked me to present an introduction for this book, I was humbled, grateful and overwhelmed by the privilege of being part of such a significant piece of work. It has been an honour and inspirational opportunity to work collaboratively with Kerrie and the other contributors to the book. I have always been drawn to Kerrie's genuine love for people and desire to connect in a non-intrusive, pure and authentic way. Among her many qualities is the smile with which she greets her audience whether she is speaking with one person or a room full of people. When she is engaging with you, it feels like you are talking to the girl next door.

The phrase 'Cheering you on' has been embedded in me since the first time I met Kerrie. Her desire to champion people into their area of passion makes her more than suited to write about building confidence. In Kerrie I have observed an authentic display of what she puts out there. Not only is she knowledgeable but her thirst for knowledge and value for quality has meant a dedicated amount of time and effort has gone into getting the people together with varied life experiences that offer a richness for the readers. Not only are there authentic conversations, but there is a passion for life and vulnerability that will allow room for that common human hunger to connect.

I have known Kerrie both personally and professionally over a number of years, and I was excited when I heard that she was writing yet another book about connecting to strangers. I wondered what else there was to say about the topic given how well the previous one was done. However, once I spoke to Kerrie and listened to what the book was about, I was intrigued once again by her genius.

The first time I came across Kerrie's book title, DO Talk to Strangers, I marvelled at the brilliance of it all as I could not think of a more suited person to write about such a topic. This book is well thought out, encouraging and will be a good read for anyone who wishes to expand their ability to connect with other people in a deeper, more meaningful manner. When I heard the subtitle of the book, How to Connect With Anyone, Anywhere, I was impressed once again by Kerrie's ability to connect to the real-life issues people struggle with, in a simple and non-threatening manner while delivering a powerful message filled with hope for those in need of change.

The unique strength of this book is that it goes beyond the idea of speaking to strangers to connect but rather it adds an intentionality and focus into addressing issues of anxiety, it helps people build confidence and it focuses on a larger vision that goes beyond the momentary connection of meeting a stranger.

Although anxiety disorders are beyond the scope of this book, this book offers people the opportunity to look at it through a different lens. It offers the opportunity to explore various day-to-day experiences of anxiety in the context of engaging with strangers and the positive experiences and lessons that can come out of those interactions. In its most severe form, anxiety can be debilitating. The stories outlined in the pages of this book and how people were able to come out on the other side of those experiences, are a road map to navigate day to day struggles.

This book appeals to me because I grew up as an anxious child who lacked confidence in a lot of areas. However, there was always a part of me that knew there was more out there and I could do more if only I was not so fearful. I looked forward to the day when I would get out of my shell and find my voice which would then allow me to cheer others on as Kerrie would put it. As you read through each of the stories, you get a glimpse of how people overcome everyday challenges and how growth and confidence flow on from that.

With increased confidence, it's only inevitable that one will make a greater difference in their world. I strongly believe that this book will go far beyond what Kerrie has imagined for it, not only because it speaks into real-life issues and experiences but because the message it carries offers freedom for people to be their authentic self and not have to try so hard to connect with other human beings.

Unami Magwenzi,
Psychologist, Perth, Australia

WELCOME AND WHY

Kerrie Phipps

I've spent much of my life feeling incredibly inadequate. Not quite - or not nearly enough. Not educated enough. Not intelligent enough. And definitely not eloquent enough.

And yet I've become an international speaker, accredited coach, and writer - for magazines, e-books, a growing number of co-authored books and five of my own.

With great trepidation, but a sense that it was a perfect fit, I commenced my International Coach Federation (ICF) accredited coach training in 2004 and immersed myself in every course available for the next 7 years, which gave me the opportunity to converse with world renowned neuroscientists, and doing selfie videos with CEOs and HR executives of Fortune 500 companies. That was back in the day before livestreaming was an option - when you'd record a video on a little camera and plug it into your laptop, edit, render and upload to Facebook or YouTube!

Did I do any of these things because I was confident? Not at all, although that was the general assumption by many. I was driven to learn - and use what I learned to make a difference. I felt privileged to connect with such incredible leaders. I also felt undeserving of the opportunities I had, which is possibly what also drove me - besides the joy of connecting and sharing - to share all I could.

I wanted people to know that, if it was possible for me to push beyond the limitations and expectations of others, plus my self-imposed limitations, it's possible for them too. I realised that it's not always the most driven, ambitious and confident people that win.

Reflecting on my diverse career I now see there were many times I resisted a promotion, or time in the spotlight. The praise or elevation from leaders also came with criticism and dissension amongst teams, individuals who didn't understand, or didn't like the decisions of leaders. Perhaps they didn't see the potential and/or strengths decision-makers saw in me, but only my inadequacies - which I was certainly aware of.

In a particularly tricky situation, I was honoured to be asked, but reluctant to take on a role I knew someone else wanted, and expected to be asked. I would have been so happy to walk away, or stay in the shadows, supporting whoever took on the role. Because I didn't want it. I didn't want the emotional and relational fallout.

If you'd asked me what I was afraid of, I wouldn't have seen myself as hiding. I remember a newspaper article about my first book in 2008 where I was asked that question. My response was something like: 'I can't think of anything at the moment - if I realise I'm afraid of something, then I have to face it and do it.'

I've grown up tackling physical challenges head on, like obstacle courses, parasailing, rock climbing, abseiling, riding motorbikes and horses. So when I've felt afraid of one of these challenges, I've done a basic safety check, and stepped in despite the fear. As my dad shared recently, 'We do dangerous things carefully'.

However, with a lack of self-awareness of less-obvious fears, I've run from the emotional challenges, assuming I was a brave person because of my upbringing and practical accomplishments. Becoming brave emotionally isn't easy; it is an ongoing learning journey.

The past few years I've found myself saying - from the stage, on social media, via text and short videos, and to many people personally - 'You make a bigger difference than you know.' I say this over and over as I need to remind them - and myself - that, 'Your voice matters'.

Your contribution matters. Your life matters.

I often receive messages of gratitude that remind me of how my life matters, that what I've considered my clumsy offerings, have made a difference. Sometimes people express that my words to them were 'a lifesaver' in personal or professional situations.

Words are powerful. At times words are literally life-saving to someone on a path of self-destruction or deep depression, as I was as a young teen. Many people encouraged me, challenged and inspired me to make better choices, helping me see that my life and contributions have value.

You know the power of words yourself if someone has made a comment or perhaps written a note that has lifted your spirits or given you an insightful perspective.

Since publishing DO Talk to Strangers: How To Connect With Anyone, Anywhere, in 2014, I've shared many reasons for talking to strangers, such as you could

- learn something new
- make a new friend

- have a great adventure
- save a life

I spoke to an audience of aspiring and professional speakers one night in Sydney. The MC introduced me and my book by sharing a powerful story. He and his family escaped a civil war in his home country when a stranger, driving away from the conflict, stopped to pick them up in his car and sped away, saving all of their lives.

We remember dramatic stories like these, however this book covers all kinds of moments in life that could appear mundane to an outsider, but to the recipient of the connection, the results can be significant. So if it occurs to you to do something kind, just do it.

For example, a potentially mundane moment occurred in a friend's cafe. A customer came in looking like he could benefit from a smile, so my friend gave him the requested coffee and said, 'No charge, mate'. The customer returned a week later, to tell the barista of his unknowing intervention. That day he had made the decision to end his life, and was on his way home to do it when he stopped for a final coffee.

A simple coffee, a small act of kindness and generosity can speak volumes.

Many times, when people simply do what feels like the right thing in the moment, the significance of the action doesn't occur to them. We process so much unconsciously, and affect each other at an unconscious level.

You'll notice some stories of simple words of encouragement and support in these pages.

I hope this book is a reminder to you that your moments of connection, especially when you're simply in the moment, doing 'the right thing' can mean so much to someone. It won't always be the person you think you're helping. So many times people have commented on witnessing small acts of kindness from a distance and it's restored their 'faith in humanity'. Your life is an example to others more than you know. Let your light shine - for your own joy and those around you.

That's it. I encourage you to be open to choose what feels like 'the right thing' in the moment, the pause, the indication of care, of courtesy or patience, rather than choosing the more convenient path of looking away and continuing with your plans. When we pause our plans for a moment to help someone or show kindness, the buzz we get makes up for lost minutes, adding value to our own life as well as the lives of others. And how many minutes might we lose trying to save time? Sometimes the energy put into avoiding a social situation can drain you even more. When we turn away from an opportunity to help, we might feel guilty or ashamed that we didn't step in - so there goes your energy for a while.

If we increase our self-awareness and pay attention to our intuition as we engage with the world around us, we can live with a sense of positivity, joy, contribution and togetherness. I hope this book helps you see that whatever thoughts you might have about connecting with people, whether you're daunted or inspired, others will feel this way at times too. You are not alone!

As you enjoy the following stories by my friends around the world, you may notice variations of spelling and some unfamiliar phrases. We have included these as written by the contributor, so you'll see British and American spelling throughout. This is not an editing error. While on the subject of editing … I've noticed my tendency, a human tendency to edit, fix, or improve. Our inner judge tries to line up the world with our way of seeing things. Have you ever noticed the urge to correct someone's pronunciation? You might hear someone's accent and repeat their word or phrase with your own accent, along with a comment (internally or aloud) such as, 'This is how we say it here'. They might appreciate your help, but they might also be exhausted by trying to fit in.

What if we accept people as they are, and only if they ask for help to adapt, then offer our suggestions? We grow up in an environment of being schooled, then take any opportunity to school people ourselves. Permission is essential. It's covered in more detail in DO Talk to Strangers where I introduced the ASKING model, but I think you'll understand the essence of this if you've ever been given unwanted advice.

We mention a few travel stories and these might feel a little unrelatable if your location is restricted right now, yet the essence of them can be related to simply 'traveling through life'. When our physical location doesn't change, we still have the opportunity to take our thinking in a fresh direction. Often this happens because of an encounter with someone - whether by an actual conversation, their words on a screen or in a book, or an encounter with yourself of course. Connecting with yourself, hearing yourself and knowing yourself is essential to connecting with others successfully.

The idea for this book has been brewing for some time now, as I am always meeting people who love sharing their stories of talking to strangers. Our world has always needed more compassion, empathy and practical support, and this is so evident now. We're inundated with news of isolation, devastation, division, rage, and despair.

Crisis, when met with compassion and empathy, is more manageable. A sense of connection can help us get through, reframing our thinking to look for opportunities even in the darkest places.

Stories are crucial to share as we gain encouragement and learn from them. We make sense of them when we have the beginning, middle and end, or we fill in the gaps with assumptions. In momentary connections with strangers, we often don't know the outcome, which is why we might disregard the importance of a small act of kindness. We might assume that it doesn't matter. This book is to remind you that your smallest contributions to society have value - and it's totally worth it to Keep Going!

As we prepared to go to print, reviewing our layout plans, I picked up a copy of DO Talk to Strangers, published in 2014, to refer to the final pages. I was stunned to find these words - which I've already written above, 'You make a bigger difference than you know'. It's a core theme of this book, and I hope it reminds you that your kindness is worth the effort. I've clearly been brewing this message for longer than I'd realised.

Let's celebrate connection, kindness and empathy, in every corner of the globe.

'I define connection as the energy that exists between people when they feel seen, heard, and valued; when they can give and receive without judgment; and when they derive sustenance and strength from the relationship.' **Brene Brown**

HOW TO TALK TO STRANGERS

How to write a 'how to'? I've grappled with this for months, no, years. It's an ongoing conversation that we need to work out continually and individually, as we are all unique, and every connection we make with others is unique in that moment. However, we can help each other to be better connectors. This book has been written to help you with your journey, and as you read the stories of our contributors, we hope you see yourself in these pages - and far beyond in your day to day connecting.

As humans, we love a good 'how to'. We want to simplify the complex, we explore the best and/or easiest ways of doing anything we want to learn or improve.

So there is a 'how to' - and I love helping people to personalise it. There are six steps in the ASKING Model, which I developed as a starting point in, DO Talk to Strangers, How to Connect With Anyone, Anywhere. This has been a great help to thousands of readers around the world, and I regularly receive messages from people in various countries who have found the ASKING Model to be 'a lifesaver' in a variety of situations. They tell me that they've picked up the book again for a quick reminder before going somewhere, reviewing the ASKING Model. Some carry the little ASKING card in their wallet. If you'd like one, please let me know!

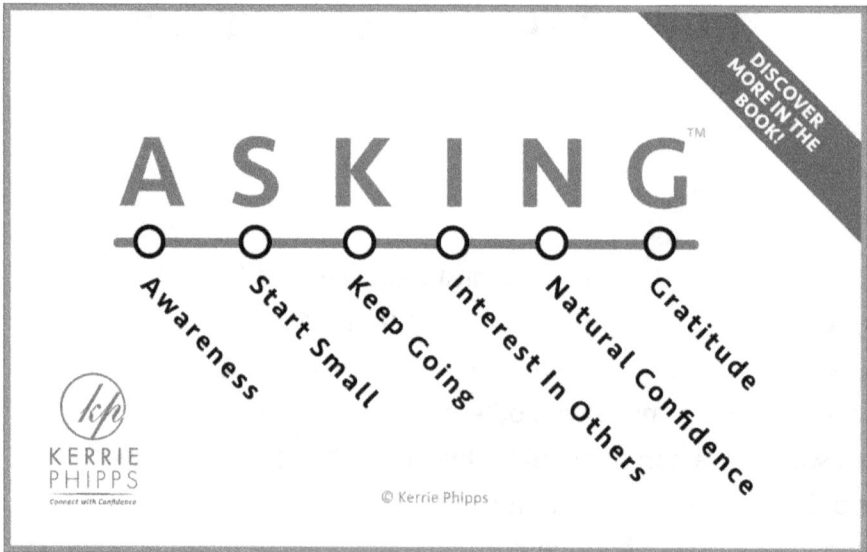

ASKING™

DISCOVER MORE IN THE BOOK!

Awareness · Start Small · Keep Going · Interest In Others · Natural Confidence · Gratitude

KERRIE PHIPPS
Connect with Confidence

© Kerrie Phipps

Awareness *(of self and others)*
Am I nervous? Let it go! How can I serve?

Start Small
Smile and step out of the comfort zone

Keep Going
Ask questions like "What did you enjoy most about...?"

Interest in Others
Make the choice to tune in and really listen

Natural Confidence
Be yourself and discuss positive things

Gratitude
Look for ways to acknowledge others

Connect With Confidence!
For more great resources visit www.kerriephipps.com

OUT NOW!

DO talk to strangers

As with anything worthwhile, we start with awareness, and move forward with honesty. Sometimes a 'how to' is a simple 1,2,3. A recipe can be followed to create the same cake every time.

Connecting with people is never going to be so straightforward, but so much more rewarding. Even if your business is famous for cake; it is people who buy it, eat it, share it, and talk about it. We can't do life without people, even if that might feel like an easier option at times.

This book is designed to walk with you in life, to hold your hand as you step into more opportunities to talk to strangers, to connect with people in a wide variety of unique situations, at times helping or being helped, and sharing the joy or challenges of a moment.

At times it's possibly building on the connection, or meeting for such a fleeting time, and potentially never meeting again.

So why do I use the word stranger? And what does it mean? If you tell a story of a person you see in the supermarket, your listener or reader wonders if you know the person, so 'stranger' is more specific. Your listener/reader realises, 'Oh, I see someone who's not yet known'. We don't know anything about them yet. It's simply a descriptor, no judgement attached. And that's one of the wonderful things about strangers, you can engage in conversation with them without judgement. You can tell them that you're thinking of studying nursing, or engineering or archaeology, and they're not attached to the outcome like someone close to you might be, they're less likely to have a strong opinion. Or it really won't affect them.

A friend or family member usually can't help being impacted by your choices, or your ideas, and they're listening to you with a focus of how it might affect them, and what they think you should do.

A stranger is less invested in what you do, unless they have an agenda, like wanting to sell you something - which is possibly related to one of your ideas - so if you're not interested you can thank them for their time and move on. You're less concerned with what a stranger thinks of your decision. Discussing ideas with people who matter to you can be challenging, especially if they have strong opinions. The lack of judgment and freedom to think aloud is one of the joys of talking to strangers that people share with me.

Every story in this book is unique, just as your stories and experiences are. Some interactions with strangers aren't great - but probably offer an opportunity for some kind of valuable learning. Many, many interactions with strangers, or witnessing strangers reaching out to others, are so rewarding. This is why the Facebook group, The Kindness Pandemic and other kindness related groups are very popular. We love discovering the beauty in other people. It gives us hope. As many people say of small moments of interaction, 'It restored my faith in humanity'.

Did you realise that your pause to help someone, to let them go ahead of you in a queue, could be their good news story? You could be the reason their faith in humanity is restored. This doesn't happen because you make it happen. It happens when you allow it to happen, when you're open to the invitation to participate in life with an open heart.

PART ONE

Decreasing Anxiety

BEING HELPED

I asked my friends to reflect on moments when a sense of anxiety decreased, or evaporated, because of a word or gesture from a stranger. If you don't think of yourself as an anxious person you might forget about these moments, but they happen to us all.

Sometimes we might go about our day with an undercurrent of anxiety, or we simply find ourselves inconvenienced, but layered upon other inconvenient moments this can become unbearable. Uncertainty and worry keep us stalled, and a simple recommendation or encouragement can make our day - or have a lifelong effect!

So, next time you're offering a little help, word of encouragement or kindness, know that it is worth it! You could be making a much bigger difference than you'd imagined.

CONOR O'MALLEY - Australia

11 April 2006, on a Qantas flight back to the UK, I was anxious at take-off.

After two days in Melbourne, following a series of interviews and a verbal offer of a job, for the biggest change in my career, I had some concerns. One of my concerns, that both Paula, my wife and I shared, was where to send the children to school.

I was sitting next to a young man, who, when I shared this concern, told me he had gone to a private school in the East of Melbourne. We discussed the private schools in the East of Melbourne, and he ended up writing them all down on a Qantas napkin for me to research when in the UK. Later in the flight, I was talking to a stewardess who, when I shared the concern, told me she had gone to a private school in the Bayside area. I asked her if she would write those schools on another Qantas napkin, she did.

Following these two encounters with strangers, I felt a sense of peace that moving to Australia was possible and one of our core concerns could be taken care of with these two napkins. Our children eventually went to one of those schools on the napkins, and I still have those napkins and treasure them.

My learning in this experience is, it is okay to share your concerns with a stranger because they may well have insights and knowledge to help you find peace or acceptance with your concern.

KATIE SWANSON - United States Of America/Vietnam

My husband and I were 10 months into our European-Asian backpacking trip when the Coronavirus pandemic really caught up to us in Vietnam. We were in Ho Chi Minh City, Vietnam, and in a matter of about 48 hours, the town became eerily quiet and shuttered as businesses were forced to close to contain the spread. We don't speak Vietnamese and were feeling anxious about our decision to stay in Vietnam to wait it out.

We went to a restaurant that had become our favorite and the owner, a young French man, came over to talk to us. We expressed our fears and uncertainty over whether or not we should find a place in Vietnam to wait it out or … what? We had no idea what we should do. He encouraged us to find a smaller city in Vietnam to wait it out, that staying in quarantine there would be safer than travelling. As we were talking, a fellow business owner came to the restaurant. He owned an Irish pub down the street and was forced by the government to close - on Saint Patrick's Day of all days! He came by to commiserate with his friend and we all ended up sharing several beers on the patio. It was so grounding to have that moment of conversation and fellowship during a time of such upheaval and uncertainty.

SIMON JACOBS - United Kingdom

I am usually quite a 'cool customer', most of the time, and it does take rather a lot to fluster me. However, this hasn't always been the case.

I think my earliest memory of experiencing the help of another to diminish my fears was when I was about 14 years old and I got the tip of my finger trapped and crushed in a fire door whilst at school.

Not wanting to go into too much gruesome detail, let's just say the end of my finger looked somewhat flatter than it did before and there was quite a lot of 'mess' in the surrounding area.

There must have been heaps of adrenaline coursing through my body at this point as I didn't and don't remember feeling any pain, just shock and panic. My PE teacher leapt into action without flinching and rushed me to the reception, where he wrapped my finger tightly in a makeshift bandage and proceeded to call an ambulance.

Had he not reacted so quickly and effectively, I firmly believe I would have spiralled, stressed and passed out. Minutes later the ambulance arrived, and this is where I met yet another calm and deeply competent individual. The paramedic was methodical and had an incredible 'bedside' manner. Without missing a beat, she was distracting me from any possible pain and keeping me buoyant throughout our journey to the hospital.

In the days following, I found myself reflecting on how impressed and thankful I was to those two specific people.

Oh, and they managed to save the tip of my finger!

UNAMI MAGWENZI - Australia

I have been pregnant and given birth four times, and each pregnancy has come with its own unique challenges. My last two children were born via Caesarean section and unfortunately, after the birth of my 4th child, I had complications, where I lost a lot of blood and was told I might need an iron infusion. Initially, I managed to remain composed as I trusted that things would improve. However, as the hours passed, and I continued to lose more blood, I began to worry. I didn't quite know what was happening to my body, but it felt odd. I was in unfamiliar territory and felt like my body was betraying me. I wondered, 'How have I ended up here, why can I not just have an uneventful pregnancy or delivery?'.

My first pregnancy involved a near-drowning when I was 6 months pregnant, my second one involved the baby being born on the living room floor, my third child was born with parts of her liver outside her body, and now this. The nurses who were attending to me were caring towards me. There was one in particular who took hold of my hand and reassured me that I was going to be okay. Despite the confusion I felt, I held on to her softly spoken and tender words and felt loved by someone who's name I can't even recall. That one gesture was special, and it made me appreciate nurses even more. It's like she knew what I needed in that moment and gave me just the right dose of it.

Take away: You can never underestimate the power of a gesture in feeding someone hope in their time of need. Do not be afraid to speak words of comfort as you may be surprised at how meaningful simple words might be.

SERENE SENG - Singapore

It was a small town in South Korea whose only attraction was tombs. I was with a history geek, so tombs we came to see. How small was the town? We couldn't find any hotels listed in all the guidebooks, and learned the only bus to town goes once a day and arrives late in the evening. We got on anyway, expecting to find accommodation near the bus station. As we rolled into town, we could see all the shops closed, and no guest houses anywhere. No one at the bus station spoke a word of English. We had nowhere to sleep or eat dinner so we started to wander around hoping for something. Then we saw 'Tourist Information Centre'.

By now we knew most small Korean towns catered only to domestic travel, so the centre staff likely didn't speak English either. But we were desperate, so we went in anyway.

There, a young man took one look at us and said, 'The centre closes in five minutes.' At this point, we didn't care how rude it was. We were just ecstatic to find someone who spoke English! We told him we needed a hotel room and dinner. 'Ok, wait five minutes', he responded. 'What?', we asked, 'You close in five minutes.' 'Yes,' he said with a smile. So, we awkwardly waited.

After he closed the centre, he took us on foot to a love hotel. Yes, the only hotel in town was a love hotel. Happily, it was a swanky, new, and very stylish love hotel. We checked in while we all pretended not to realise it was a love hotel. The young man was obviously embarrassed he knew it so well. He waited for us, and then walked us to the deserted main street, and up a dark flight of rickety stairs. He pushed open a door that had no signboard, and inside was a deserted dining hall. He spoke in Korean to the lady proprietor and she seated us at a great table and handed us a menu in Korean with no pictures. We looked at the menu; we looked at the lady. The young man joined our table with a smile. 'What do you want to eat?' he said. 'Why don't you join us for dinner and order for us?' we invited. He gladly agreed, and we had the most delicious Korean meal we had ever had in our lives. We still talk about it to this day!

We also learnt a lot more about the tombs than any guidebook ever said, as he regaled us with the colourful history of the town. He also gave us directions on how to walk to the tomb. The town was so small, you could get everywhere by walking. When the bill came, our eyes popped at how low it was. Then past midnight, the young man walked us back to our hotel, and we never saw him again.

We've travelled for years to many countries, but this was a night we still remember decades later. All because a stranger went out of his way to share a town he knew and loved.

ANUPAMA SINGAL - Singapore

Standing in the shadows of a pillar, I gazed out. A bit amused with my reaction, but also a bit anxious. So much colour was greeting my eyes that I was feeling a bit out of place. I had just walked into my new college in Delhi and was feeling a bit apprehensive if this nerdy engineer would be accepted by a bunch of creative people who were into fashion education.

Having studied in an engineering college for four years, where there were only eleven girls in my batch, I had become accustomed to the 'typical boys colours' - whites, blues and greys. It was a real shock to see so much colour, hear so much (feminine) laughter and see happy, smiling faces chatting to each other. I was so engrossed in observing everyone and thinking about which group to walk towards, that I almost jumped out of my skin when I got a light tap on my shoulder.

'Kya hua? Bahut pareshaan lag rahi ho!' a lilting voice asked me in Hindi. ('What happened? You are looking very tense!')

I just blurted, 'I am so happy to see so many girls!'

The moment the words left my mouth, I thought how baffled the other girl would be - because this was 25 years ago, and in India, a girl saying she is happy to see so many girls would sound a bit strange to another girl. Rightly so! She immediately stepped back and gave a queer head-to-toe look and said, 'Really? And WHY is THAT?'

I quickly explained how I had not been used to seeing a lot of girls on campus as I was from an engineering class of 2 girls and 40 boys. Thank God she asked me and I explained because otherwise my happiness at seeing other girls could have been misconstrued.

But, as soon as we started talking, not knowing each other at all and suddenly discussing intimate feelings of joy, apprehension and excitement, without even knowing each other's names, the feeling that I was going to be being judged fell away. She was so intrigued about my experience of studying in a class of forty boys where she had come from an 'all-girls' college', that we were comparing notes and experiences freely and easily. She told me how, just moments before she noticed me looking tense, she herself had been standing at the same spot looking at the boys and thinking - 'Thank God! I am finally going to be able to make some boyfriends!'.

We started laughing so much and I felt all my tension dissolve as we properly introduced ourselves and promised to teach each other how to make friends with the gender that we were not used to dealing with. Then, giggling and chatting we walked into the building suddenly feeling more joyful and confident because each of us had found someone we could help and get help from. I am still friends with her and we laugh about how we could have possibly missed having this friendship, had she not approached me.

This is what I feel communication is all about. If we drop the apprehension that someone is going to judge us and just simply share from the heart, reaching out to help someone or make them more comfortable, we may find that the big story we were building up in our head is just that - a story.

ANNA SHEPPARD - Australia

There have been more times than I can count that a stranger has reassured me or shown up with just the right message at the right time. Call it divinity, or call it the final piece of the puzzle, either way, when you start paying attention and counting these interactions, it's hard to put it all down to coincidence.

As a speaker and founder in the leadership space, my daily interactions are with strangers and colleagues who are keen to learn, develop and make an impact. We discuss what motivates them and use this to make them kinder and more impactful as leaders. I am a fast-paced thinker, so what I've consciously worked on is my ability to slow down and prioritise listening when it's needed. Listening and creating psychological safety is such a powerful tool in understanding and supporting others. A wise woman (and a stranger, actually) once told me, 'You have two ears and one mouth. Learn to listen twice, and more than you speak.' I carry this with me everywhere I go.

Over the COVID period, we (Bambuddha Group) listened to what people needed and then responded with a free support program for business leaders and the community. We called it the Bambuddha Boost, offering advice and tips each morning to provide both reassurance and practical resources that would educate and empower watchers.

We also facilitated Friday Cuddles, where groups of leaders met each Friday and offered peer-to-peer support and just general conversation. Just by the very act of giving and consistently showing up each morning and each week, we created, alongside our members, an environment for mutual encouragement and care.

I didn't have the best start in life and from time to time, my overactive amygdala (a part of the brain that helps us experience emotions) has left me feeling a little wobbly and unbalanced. But through self-observation, kindness, advice and research, I've better understood the cycles and stories we tell ourselves (that can feel like we've got no control over) and how they can send us around in circles. Our brains are so powerful, and they love to test the boundaries. Creating a toolkit for wellness that works for you is the key to finding balance and walking the emotional tightrope. This includes surrounding myself with people who empower me to find solutions to my challenges. Often, these people started out as strangers and became friends through our shared experience, our stories of resilience and impact. These friends remind me every day to be grateful, to be humble and to be kind.

However, I think it's important to state that we cannot look to others to solve all our issues. For a long period of time, I would agonise over my fears and problems and seek external reassurance, burying and not solving the fears and problems themselves. So when I started to realise that this mindset was reinforcing the cycle of anxiety, I knew I needed to make changes. I would say that helping others find the confidence and the solution within themselves is the biggest kindness. The reality is, everyone likes to hear that 'everything is going to be ok' (especially in times of great uncertainty). But taking that extra bit of time to ask gentle questions, to unshackle someone's inaction or unwillingness to change and find the reassurance within themselves, is a beautiful thing.

PATRICK GALVIN - United States of America

When I arrived in a small Spanish town as an exchange student from the United States, I felt lonely because the local high school students seemed standoffish. When I shared these feelings with my host mother, she reached out to a friend and asked that she introduce me to her son who attended my school. He graciously introduced me to his friends. In a matter of weeks, I went from having no friends to having dozens. They introduced me to delicious local food, regional art and music, fun local hikes, moviemaking, and so much more. Through long conversations with my new friends, I gained wonderful insights into myself, and the differences between the United States and Spain. I also learned that the townspeople weren't unfriendly, rather, they were simply wary of strangers.

Nearly 40 years later, I am still good friends with the students I got to know at my Spanish high school. We have been providing moral support to one another during the pandemic, thanks to video conferencing technology and text messaging that we could not even have imagined in high school. My life is so much richer thanks to the many welcoming people I met in Spain.

KALEY CHU - Australia

This was something that occurred regularly in 2018 when I embarked on a journey to have lunch with 100 strangers in one year.

I suffered a lot of anxiety during the journey, especially in the early stages - but to understand why, you first need to know the backstory.

In 2005, I moved from Hong Kong to Melbourne, to start university. After I finished my studies, I decided to stay permanently in Australia. That's not to say I felt comfortable in Australia. Even though I loved the country, I felt like a fish out of water. All my friends were from Hong Kong. My husband was from Hong Kong. And I felt anxious every time I had to socialise with non-Asian Australians, especially in a business context.

At the same time, I was just drifting along, going nowhere in life.

Each of those problems - anxiety, timidness and underachievement - were linked.

Matters came to a head in late 2017, after I'd started a new job - in sales of all things! I was on probation and my boss took me along to my first client meeting. For the first hour, I was too nervous to talk. The client (a non-Asian Australian) then asked me a question.

Guess what I said in reply?

Nothing.

No words came out of my mouth. I didn't know what to say. I was too nervous.

Can you imagine how humiliated I felt?

It was the lowest point of my life, but it turned out to be a blessing in disguise. I knew I needed to solve this problem that had been building for 12 years, ever since I'd moved to Australia. I realised a big problem needed a big solution. So I decided to do something big, really big. I decided to have lunch with 100 strangers in 2018.

My first lunch was excruciating. The person I met was friendly and kept trying to draw me into conversation, but I was so nervous, I could barely talk.

The next few lunches were also really hard. I wanted to quit. However, I knew that would send a terrible message to my two young children. I wanted them to learn all of us can achieve great things in life if we aim high and persevere when the going gets tough. So I realised I had to walk my talk.

Do you know what made it easier to continue?

It was the encouragement of the strangers I was meeting.

When they heard my story, they were so supportive. They told me they admired what I was doing and urged me to keep going. Their encouragement gave me the strength to go on.

Of course, we rely on our friends and family for moral support, but we underestimate the impact strangers can have on our lives - and the impact we can have on the lives of strangers. When a stranger offers the right type of emotional support at the right time, it can give us the strength we didn't realise we had.

GANESH SOMWANSHI - Singapore/India

The year 2020 has been witnessed by everyone across the globe with varied emotions due to the pandemic. One of the emotions I woke up with one fine day was, 'Is the world coming to an end?' The question was hovering in my mind for a long time during the day, and my inquisitive mind kept troubling me. I sat down at the corner of the snack shop in my Singapore neighbourhood to have a Teh C (Tea with Milk) which is my favourite evening snack drink.

There was a lady, maybe in her late 70s, who came and sat in front of me and we started chit-chatting. The topic indeed was about the pandemic, the global crisis. We discussed unemployment and about people stuck in a whirlwind of varied emotions, mostly negative. As I started opening up to her, I shared the daunting question I had woken up with: 'Is the world coming to an end?'

She was completely calm and composed, and answered my question, 'Of course not.' She added, 'The bad world is coming to an end and we should embrace the new beginning with open arms'. Her thoughts enlightened and encouraged me to give back to society.

I am sure she was God's messenger who healed me instantly.

JULIE WOODS - New Zealand

Being blind, encouragement and kindness from strangers has often come by way of gestures. Whether it's the offer of help at an intersection or in a women's toilet, I've had countless people come up to me to guide me. My husband Ron, has always been reluctant to accompany me into women's toilets, whether in Dunedin or Denmark, China or Cambodia, on countless occasions I have been taken by the hand by a female stranger, guiding me into a cubicle, waiting until I reappear, position me in front of the washbasin, guide me to the soap and hand towels and then reverse the entrance, only to deposit me back to Ron. I can't tell you how many women around the world have assisted me at a time when entering a foreign toilet has been my challenge. It made me feel less anxious and knowing that someone took time out of their day to help me, made me feel valued. I learned from those situations that help is always available; all you have to do is ask!

COEN TAN - Singapore

7am, 23 March 2018, O'Hare International Airport, Chicago.

I had arrived on a 5:30am flight from Cleveland, only to be left waiting for an hour at the baggage claim but did not receive my baggage.

It was the final leg of my trip, but I was to spend another three more days in wintry conditions in Chicago. Therefore, not receiving my toiletries and my change of clothes was very disconcerting indeed!

I approached the baggage ground staff at O'Hare Airport and met Sandra, who was sweet and reassuring. She asked me questions and took down the information with empathy and relaxed light-heartedness. She made several calls to try to locate my missing luggage. With every call she made, every step she took, she would inform me what she was doing. So that made me feel very reassured.

Eventually, she was able to track my baggage to Columbus. When she heard that they were planning to send my baggage back to Chicago via Denver, which meant a 6 hour-round trip, she expressed real concern and placed several calls to ground staff in Columbus, to see if they could find a different route so that I could get my bag before the final delivery at 8pm. Eventually, her efforts were in vain and my luggage arrived the next morning, but the dedication to her job represented a high point moment to me.

I can imagine what a thankless job she has, standing for hours every day watching bag after bag circulating with nary an eventful occurrence, except for angry complaints or anxious passengers like me. However, when called into action, she rose to the occasion.

People going about their jobs with love, completely dedicated to doing the best job in service of others. That, to me, is divine.

LYNDON PHIPPS - Australia

I first met Katie and Andy from Oklahoma on my second day of walking the Camino Frances (The Way of St. James), not far out of Roncesvalles which is the first town in Spain after I crossed over the Pyrenees starting in St. Jean Pied de Port in France. We walked together for an hour or so until Espinal-Aurizberri where we parted ways. We enjoyed each other's company and encouragement as we hiked through the rain, but there was no certain expectation of meeting again, as our timelines were very different.

43 days later, I was returning to Santiago De Compostela from Muxía where I finished my pilgrimage. Arriving in Santiago de Compostela in Spain for the first time after walking over 800km is … unexplainable.

Needless to say, I am overwhelmed with emotion just writing this and having difficulty seeing the words through the tears my heart is squeezing out of my eyes.

After 2 days resting in Santiago, I walked another 3 days to Muxía, where I spent more time in contemplation and catching up with other pilgrims, until I knew this part of my journey was over. I had walked across an entire country. As I watched the sun nestle itself into the Atlantic ocean, painting the sky and water with its fiery fingers, my heart and soul settled into a comfortable agreement. It was time to rejoin the Camino of life. I wanted to go home.

I caught the bus back to Santiago and realised on the way that the friends who I'd made along the way had gone home to their respective countries. New pilgrims would be arriving in the huge square at Santiago, having similar experiences to those I had the week before.

I found this quite distressing, as I could feel the resignation of my journey being over. I was crashing from the high I had been on for so long, and I just did not want to be alone in Santiago. It felt like the worst place I could be. I whispered a prayer.

'Dear God. Please let there be someone I know there. I don't want to be alone in a place of such celebration.'

I trudged from my Alburge (pilgrim accommodation) to the post office through the square with its newly arriving pilgrims; my melancholy a clear juxtaposition to their adulation.

On my way back to the Alburge, as I turned the corner into the square I saw ... possibly familiar faces, 'Do I know you?' I said tentatively.

'Yes! Katie and Andy, from Oklahoma,' was the response.

I embraced them with relief. My prayer had been answered.

We agreed to meet later that day and - over pizza, wine and conversation, the depth of which you may only ever experience on the Camino - we became friends, even though we'd only known each other for several hours. We've kept in touch and you can read some of their experiences in Katie's stories in this book.

CATHY JOHNSON - Singapore

When I was in high school, I worked at a job at one of the major department stores in Charlotte, North Carolina. After school, I would take the bus for about a 30-minute ride downtown to my job. One afternoon, it was pouring rain. I don't remember ever experiencing rain that hard, but I did have an umbrella, and I was running towards the bus stop when I saw the bus coming.

I ran as hard as I could, breathing hard, trying to catch it before it moved away. But as I ran beside the bus, it began to slowly pull away and either the driver didn't see me or he was in a hurry.

I missed the bus, but not only that, the wind and rain became fiercer. All of a sudden my umbrella was blown upside down so it was convex instead of concave - not how an umbrella can keep the rain off the person holding it. And next, it broke so that it wouldn't ever be able to protect from rain. It was ruined, and I felt ruined as well.

I had run so hard and lost the race, my umbrella had flipped and the rain was now drenching me. My umbrella was broken so I couldn't make it right, and as I stood there at the bus stop in the pouring rain, I felt totally dejected - devastated really, and I just started crying. I also knew since I missed the bus, I wouldn't be able to make it to work on time.

So what could I do? The rain kept pouring, thunder was deafening and I knew I couldn't just stand there. There were homes along the street, and in a moment I decided to do something I had never done. I walked up to the nearest house, climbed the steps and knocked on the door. What a risk I was taking! I had no idea who would be on the other side - it could be an axe-murderer or a child molester! And then I heard the doorknob turning, and as it slowly opened, I saw an old woman who smiled at me and said, 'Hello - come in, come in!' I began to tell her what happened with the rain, being late for work, sorry to barge in - but she stopped me and said, 'Come inside, come inside. You need to get dry and warm.'

The next few hours were some that I'll never forget. She sat me in a large, soft, comfortable 'Lazy-boy' chair in a small comfortable living room, with a warm crackling fireplace near to my chair. She insisted on placing my wet shoes and socks by the fire, and then she brought me a cup of tea. She helped me to call my work to tell them I wouldn't be able to come in and sweetly chatted with me until the rain died down and I could make my way home. After such a disturbing and worrying experience, being there with this lovely sweet woman so focused on taking care of me, I felt such a rush of gratitude - deep thankfulness for being so blessed.

MASAMI SATO - Singapore

I have an endless list of times I was lost and in trouble in the past. And there were a few that were most memorable.

Twenty-five years ago, I was studying Spanish in Guatemala and living with a homestay family. During my study break, I flew into San José, the capital city of Costa Rica, with my small backpack and less than ten dollars in my pocket. My plan was to get local currency from an ATM machine to fund my two week budget adventure there. Yet to my dismay, ATM machines failed to give me any cash. It was Saturday and banks were closed.

After 2 nights at a budget guesthouse (luckily it cost about $3 to stay at some of the cheapest accommodations then), conserving the cash by not eating, I marched to a nearby bank first thing on Monday morning. I was told my card had no use in this country. Full stop.

So … what do you do when you find yourself penniless in a country where you know no one?

As any penniless backpacker would do (?), I headed to a long-distance bus terminal and randomly took a bus to a remote region in the late afternoon, believing that people in the countryside would be more friendly and I'd be able to find a place to stay if I offered to work in exchange. I used up all the money left in my pocket to buy a ticket to a town which had a nice-sounding name.

I only discovered that this place was nearly 6 hours away on the bus when I finally reached there at night. So, stepping into a dark, unlit dirt road felt quite surreal. I wasn't even sure which direction I came from to get to this place. It looked very rural but I wasn't even sure because I couldn't see much of anything.

Sometimes, you just have to surrender. So, I started to knock on doors of small houses along the street. One by one, I encountered strangers, people who lived in those small houses. With my poor Spanish, I explained that I was a penniless Japanese traveller who was willing to do any work if they could let me stay.

I was probably a little too optimistic. Most people in this town seemed to be very 'poor' and they apologised that they didn't have space to let me stay or extra food to feed me. At least, they thought someone else in town may be able to take me in. So, they pointed me to someone else's house, then to another.

Finally, I reached this small Chinese restaurant which was already getting ready to close. The lady owner of the restaurant took me in and made me a hot plate of fried rice, saying that her son had a similar challenge when he was travelling in Europe. I suddenly remembered how hungry I was. I assure you it was the BEST fried rice I had ever eaten.

That 'holiday without money' became one of the very best times I had during my travelling days. I received so much kindness from so many people. I was even rescued by a local Red Cross team, and stayed with the leader of the unit. When I left the town, all the young people at the village headquarters of Red Cross gathered their pocket money to give to me, to send me back safely in the end. I knew they didn't have such luxury to support a silly young and poor traveller. But they were so generous and joyous. They all stood on the dirt road waving at me until the car finally turned and we couldn't see each other anymore.

I will never forget that kindness, the openness and the laughter those people shared with me.

I also never knew that just 3 years ago here in Singapore, I would walk up to a Director General of the International Committee of the Red Cross and indirectly thank him for that kindness I received from his admirable colleagues in that remote community. And as fate would have it, he eventually became my mentor and a friend too.

The unconditional kindness I received from strangers during the times of difficulty impacted me so much. And what I do today is largely influenced by those experiences.

One day, I'll go back there - to actually thank them in person.

NATHAN SHOOTER - Australia

In your moment of need, has a total stranger been there for you? If we think back, most of us have a memorable moment like that.

By now, you've read countless stories of weary travellers being reassured by the kindness of strangers. It would seem that when we're out of our comfort zone, somewhere foreign, the simple acts of service mean much more to us than they ordinarily would back home.

A few years ago, my sister and I decided to pause work, and take to the skies, Europe bound. Fast forward past Dubai, past Spain, beyond France, to our touch down in Florence, Italy.

It was cold and dark when we found ourselves trapped out the front of the airport, waiting for hours. A major bridge was closed, giving us no way to our destination. Eventually we found our way to the accommodation, only to discover the door closed and tightly locked. We were outside in the cold and dark, again.

Sometime after midnight a car drove past, stopped in the middle of the street, then reversed toward us slowly. Should we be nervous? Were they here to help? A tall silhouette emerged from the vehicle and closed the door. Help had arrived. Upon sharing our plight with this stranger, he seemed frustrated on our behalf; almost embarrassed as a local.

That night, he took a risk on us. With nothing to gain, he took the opportunity to help relieve the anxiety of total strangers.

Within minutes, he'd arranged a hotel and transport. In the early hours of the morning, we rolled our luggage through the doors of a beautiful, warm hotel because a stranger chose to use his business connections, for good.

Supporting a stranger can often feel risky and inconvenient. But what it shouldn't feel, is complicated. Serving others is at its best, when it acts quickly, and is delivered simply.

This week, let's look for an opportunity to slow down, stop, reverse, and ask how we can be of service to someone. It's a choice that might bring someone in from the cold, or even change a life.

KERRIE PHIPPS - Australia

As Lyndon walked across Spain in May/June 2019, I explored a little of Europe, being constantly reminded of the kindness of strangers and the value of practical support. I didn't feel compelled to see the tourist places, I simply wanted to be out of my comfort zone, meeting new people with vastly different worldviews to hear their stories and learn more.

I arrived in Hamburg Hauptbahnhof (central station) from a suburban station, the first of a series of five trains I had booked to Dresden. The names of all the stations listed on the boards were completely foreign to me, and I don't know when I've ever felt so bewildered.

Totally lost. I asked people nearby, 'Excuse me, do you speak English?' and several didn't, or simply shrugged and pointed. I found the information centre, where I saw people inside, behind the counter, and was stopped by a man at the door who told me it doesn't open until 10am.

'But my train leaves at 9.58am!'

He pointed down a wide corridor so I quickly followed a moving crowd, to discover more, bigger boards with more trains and times listed. I looked up at the board, down at my ticket, trying desperately to make sense of it all.

I quickly surveyed the many people around me, looking for friendly faces, and turned to a young couple nearby and asked for help. The young woman asked where I needed to go and I showed her my ticket. She quickly indicated she'd lead me and began threading her way through the crowd, deeper into the station, past many platforms. I glanced back to see her partner, he was at least 5 people behind me. I kept up with her as best I could.

She suddenly stopped and looked up at the platform number, 'This isn't it!' and began running down the stairs to the left.

I knew I had only minutes to find the train and didn't want to contemplate what would happen if I didn't make it. I had no option but to trust that her searching for my train in that moment was more informed, and likely to succeed than my own efforts.

Further down the platform, past a train, was the next platform, with the train I needed. As I stepped on board, turning to her, all I could say through my breathlessness was, 'Thank you so much! Thank you!'

She couldn't have understood how much it meant to me to make it onto that train. I was on the train with 30 seconds to spare, catching my breath and wishing I could convey my gratitude to her. I know she was happy to help, and I hope she and her partner felt that burst of joy that we often feel when we know we've made even a small difference.

This was one of the moments in which I saw the contrast in perspectives of the stranger helping someone out, and the one being helped. Helping might only take a moment, but can have a significant ripple effect. She made a bigger difference than she could've imagined. If I'd missed the train, and therefore every following connection, I would have missed the opportunity to experience the kind of learning curve that comes with being out of my comfort zone, as I had intended for this trip. I wanted my world to expand, my heart to expand, with greater empathy and understanding for others.

So much about the trip to Dresden was unexpected and significant. I stood at the end of a full carriage for the trip from Hamburg to Uelzen, then changed trains, after learning from a local how to navigate the train station quickly, as there were very few minutes between arrival and departure. As the train from Uelzen to Magdeburg had assigned seating, I found myself sharing the trip with a young Syrian refugee, who was stunned and grateful that I bought him a bottled drink as I bought myself one. He subsequently poured his heart out to me, about his devastated country, his troubled journey to Germany, his mother who remained in Syria, and his friend who he was anxious to see in the next city. He shared his professional skills that were profitable in Syria and his inability to find work in Germany, his fears for the future and lack of hope.

In Leipzig I had a good half hour to find my next train, and spent some time in the most stunning Starbucks I'd ever seen. It was located in the original first-class lounge in the beautifully restored station.

Arriving in Dresden, nearly 7 hours after departing, I was met by a new Linkedin friend Michael, who was visiting from Arizona with his wife and 19-year-old son. Michael had connected with me only weeks before, after seeing my brief Linkedin video with Frank in Singapore at Asia Professional Speakers Convention. After a few messages he called to invite me - if I accepted Frank's invitation to Germany - to come down to Dresden to meet up with them and attend a concert in the historically significant Dresden Frauenkirche.

As Michael had been intrigued by DO Talk to Strangers on my Linkedin profile, and the video conversation with Frank about traveling and connecting, rather than simply buying me a ticket as offered, he bought two, in case I met someone I wanted to invite to the concert.

I laughed and said, 'Are you putting me to the test?'

So, I looked around the town square. On the steps of the beautifully restored church, a lady sat with her bag on her lap. We didn't speak the same language, but when she realised that I was offering her a ticket as a gift, she leapt to her feet and came inside. For the next hour or more she sat entranced, mostly with her eyes closed and a smile on her face. I've never seen such bliss, and was grateful that Michael had acted so generously, and that I found the right person for his gift.

As a result of a young woman's efforts to get me to my train, I was able to experience these moments and more in Dresden for 24 hours. I then spent 24 hours in Berlin on my way back to Hamburg. This was also an important part of my journey, as I walked the streets from my hotel near Checkpoint Charlie, along the remains of the Berlin Wall, to the Brandenburg gate.

It was there I came across hundreds of people with the Syrian flag on their shoulders, which included another heartbreaking and insightful conversation with a Syrian refugee.

The young woman in Hamburg may have simply assumed she helped me catch a train in one anxious moment, but she also expanded my world and I am so grateful.

HELPING OTHERS

When roles are reversed … When have you seen your connection with someone decrease their anxiety?

I asked my friends to share moments when they've connected in a way that has put someone at ease, decreasing their anxiety or concern. Sometimes they went out intentionally to give care or encouragement, at other times it was a spontaneous, naturally occurring moment of kindness.

You might see a sense of relief on someone's face, or you go on your way, hoping you've made a difference. It's important to remember that you often won't know the outcome, or the full significance of the moment, but it's quite likely to matter more than you imagined.

PATRICK

I have been a member of the Rotary Club of Portland, Oregon (USA) for nearly eight years. When I first visited the club, a few Rotarians greeted me warmly. They asked why I was interested in joining Rotary and shared their stories with me about what they enjoyed most about belonging to the organization. These friendly conversations inspired me and played a significant role in my decision to join the club.

As an active club member, I often volunteer to serve as an official greeter. My role is to stand at the door and shake people's hands and say 'Hello' as they come into the meeting. If I am not at the door, I invite visitors to sit down at my table and have lunch with me. I'm a naturally curious person, so I ask people why they are visiting our club. These conversations often uncover interesting and longtime family connections to Rotary. People also like to share personal and professional stories about the things that they are passionate about and which motivate their commitment to community service.

Typically, in the day or two after a Rotary club meeting, I send visitors a handwritten card, email, or LinkedIn connection request thanking them for their attendance. I share something interesting we discussed and offer to answer any questions they might have. I also let them know how delighted I would be if they joined our club. I am proud to say that five current club members have told me that the warm welcome and personal follow-up that I provided was one of the important factors motivating them to join.

CONOR

As the caddy for a brilliant 17-year-old golfer in a club competition my courage to have a 'conversation for possibilities' in the moment put him at ease to execute the shot he originally saw, that was in my view a 'ten percenter'.

We were in a competition round against a player he was anxious to beat, as he knew him well. On one hole he put his drive into the trees. When we got to his ball, he saw the 'ten percent' shot of drawing it around the trees with a low 'hook' that would take the ball to the front right of the green.

After he shared what he saw, I asked him was he open to looking at other possibilities? He said he was, and we discussed options, including knocking it back onto the fairway only 10 metres to his right. After consideration, he discarded that possibility and chose to hit the 'ten percenter'.

When the ball stopped on the front right of the green and he won the hole, he shared with me that the 'conversation for possibilities' put him at ease and enabled him to really focus on the shot he initially chose and then execute it to perfection.

In hindsight, perhaps it was only a 'ten percenter' for someone of my golfing ability, not his!

Having a 'conversation for possibilities' is a great way of providing an environment for someone to be at ease with themselves, or a choice they have already made, before they take action on that choice.

JULIE

I was in Sigiriya, the 5th Century 'Fortress in the Sky', 600 feet high, a UNESCO World Heritage Site in Sri Lanka. The climb was demanding to say the least, interrupted at a half-way point where three guards stopped us to demand our tickets. Ron had only one ticket and they insisted we needed two. While we were waiting at the halfway point for our second ticket to come, a Spanish couple arrived. We asked their names; he was Joachim and she was Esperanza. Esperanza was petrified with fear of heights, and said she could not look down, and was contemplating stopping at that point.

I explained that I was blind, and suggested the solution was for her to look up, not down.

When we reached the top, we met the couple again. Esperanza was grateful for my words of encouragement saying 'I never would have made it up there without you Julie.' We found out later that Esperanza means 'hope' in Spanish, which seemed very fitting.

KATIE

When we were hiking El Camino de Santiago across Spain in 2019, we were introduced by a fellow pilgrim to a young woman who was frazzled and exhausted by trying to keep up with the group of pilgrims she had first started the hike with. She was physically exhausted, stressed out, and morale seemed low. I recognized her reluctance to accept our invitation to walk with us - not because we were strangers, but rather in admitting defeat by not being able to stay in stride with faster hikers; she had an old injury that had flared up and was causing a lot of pain and discomfort but she was so determined to keep going.

We very much embraced the 'hike your own hike' philosophy and encouraged her to let go of the need to keep up with anyone else - this journey was hers and we would support her in whatever way we could. We ended up walking together for the next 30 days, growing into our own little pilgrim family and forging a bond that will last a lifetime.

UNAMI

In my work as a Psychologist, I am often confronted with people's fears and concerns about all sorts of issues. The worries range from everyday concerns about life in general to more complicated issues such as trauma, unresolved grief, complex relationship dynamics and other difficulties they may be facing.

One of the best tools I have found in helping put people at ease, is when I 'normalise' their experience. For a lot of people going to see a Psychologist is seen as a sign of weakness. There is something about helping people realise that given their experiences, and the hard times they have been through, it makes perfect sense that they would be feeling worried, anxious or unsettled.

When I have normalised an experience for people they have given a huge sigh of relief and this has often allowed them to open up a bit more and realise that there is nothing impossible about their situation and it can be worked on.

SERENE

Morning rush hour on the underground train meant that I was squashed against the far door by a mass of human bodies. Next to me was a young man similarly squashed. For some reason I couldn't explain, I turned to look at him.

Now, this was Singapore, where nobody made eye contact, and a train of thousands was totally silent. No one spoke. So to turn to look at him was an affront.

But then when I looked at him, I realised he looked somehow crushed. He was slumped in on himself and holding himself up by his hands. Waves of despair and depression rolled off him. Before I could stop myself, I said, 'It's going to be ok. Whatever it is will pass. Time heals all wounds.'

I could tell that people stiffened around me. No one turned to look at us of course. But people were uncomfortable that I'd spoken to him. Still, the young man turned to look at my shoes, and nodded at them so I felt encouraged. I tried to say something else, but all that came to mind were platitudes and clichés.

I didn't know what to do, so I dug in my bag for a book I was reading on healing emotional trauma, and opened to a page I knew well. 'Read this', I pointed to the paragraph. He read silently for a few minutes.

The page had an exercise to do. 'So do it.' I said. He did.

In a crowded train, as people silently moved away to give us space. 'How you feel?' I asked in Singlish.

He said nothing. It was fast coming up to my stop.

'It's going to be ok you know. It'll be ok. I'm getting off at the next stop.' I said in a rush. I didn't know what else to say. He handed me back the book.

'Keep the book,' I said.

He looked up and made eye contact for the first time. He made an expression I couldn't read. 'I got to go.' I said as I made my way to the other door, 'It'll be ok.' I turned, but couldn't see him through the crowd of people.

I never saw the young man again, and I don't know to this day if I actually helped him. He never said a word to me. He only looked at me that one time. But the incident changed the way I looked at the world. I live in a 'mind your own business' society. The underlying belief is that people can deal with their own issues. And if not, their families will help them. It's considered rude to assume otherwise, and nose your way into others' private affairs.

But when I truly **looked** at the young man that day, I saw a different reality. I saw how, as Thoreau said, 'The mass of men lead lives of quiet desperation.'

And I couldn't avert my eyes after that. I became the nosey parker who would now look at a situation and ask myself, 'Is this something I should intervene in?' From abusive parents to suspicious bags, I stepped in, I called, I spoke up.

Whether this is better or worse than the old way, I don't know, but the old way wasn't something I could do anymore.

ANUPAMA

It was Deepawali time, and I had been shopping for sweets, decorations, all sorts of grocery and prayer things in Little India, Singapore. My hands were full with bags and I was standing by the road trying to hail a taxi by nodding my head. Out of the corner of my eye, I noticed a group of Europeans agitatedly talking to each other in French and sometimes in Spanish. People around them were staring and avoiding walking too close to them. Getting this kind of treatment was making them even more anxious and angry, I think.

Suddenly, one of them jumped in front of me and tried to hail a taxi - the taxi-driver slowed down and heard where they wanted to go. Then, as he saw the group approach he started shouting at them and saying 'No! No! Cannot! Cannot!' and sped away.

The group stepped back with pained expressions and again started talking amongst themselves. I was intrigued. From what I could see, they had just shown a card to him to take them to their hotel. So, I thought I should try to find out where they want to go and help them somehow.

I approached them and asked them why they were so agitated, and all of them immediately started talking to me. They had tried to hail seven taxis and the drivers would just slow down, look at them, mumble something and drive away. They told me their hotel was a fancy five-star hotel, but no one was willing to take them there. Each driver had his own way of refusing and 'shouting' in their face by saying 'Cannot, Cannot!' They asked me if it was because of their white skin or was it because their hotel had a bad reputation in Singapore or was it 'haunted' or something else? All of them had a question they were asking me at once - why did the Taxi drivers not want to take them to their hotel?

Hearing all kinds of possible explanations from them, I could not help but feel a bit amused. I put my bags down and helped them understand that their hotel was a coveted property, it was not haunted - but the drivers had been probably trying to tell them that all five of them could not go in one taxi.

Being ignorant of a simple rule which allows normal taxis to only carry four passengers in Singapore, these tourists were imagining all kinds of reasons why, for the last 40 minutes they could not hail a taxi ride and drivers would just keep driving past or rush off without giving any explanations. As I explained, and spoke to them, one by one their expressions changed and they started smiling and laughing, suddenly feeling lighter and shedding all their angst, thinking that they were being discriminated against.

It was such a joy to see them transform from a group of angry, swearing people who everyone had been staring at, to a group who were laughing freely at themselves and kicking themselves to have been such fools. One of them also admitted he had heard one of the drivers shout 'Only four! Only four!' in passing, but he didn't pay attention to what the driver was telling him. He just felt rejected and became angry.

I helped book a bigger taxi for them using Uber, and it was such a joy to see them waving at me while I saw them off before booking my own cab.

I made a mental note: 'We should talk to strangers, especially if they look like tourists and are agitated. We can all do with a little help in a foreign country … a friendly nod, an offer to chat and little support can immediately help an anxious, lost or lonely soul.'

ANNA

I have always lived my life on the cusp of anxiety and productivity, one almost fueling the other and together producing a quite hefty feeling of imposter syndrome. Yet, even so, I have a very strong intuition and moral compass. So if you, like me, often notice other people's wobbly moments, you might be wondering: how do I use my ability to see what's happening, to support this person in the moment? How do I create an environment of connection and comfort to get this person to open up?

Sometimes, the situation calls for a little more caution; a lighter hand, but an even stronger commitment to support. This is likely when something traumatic has just occurred for someone; an end of life, a sickness, or a cataclysmic life event.

I always remember this one time. It was Mother's Day, maybe 15 years ago. My family were living on a canal boat in the English countryside. These canals were built to service the cotton mills in the northwest of the UK. My family would travel from town to town, bumping into all kinds of characters along the way. My father, as someone determined not to conform to the rules of society, had decided to fit a wooden stove fire with a chimney to the top of the boat. Unfortunately, the fire was built too close to the roof tiles. And on that Mother's Day all those years ago, I arrived to find my father, mother and two of my sisters stood on the path alongside the canal with no shoes, covered in smoke and looking extremely shell-shocked. The boat had blown up, and they'd lost everything. The first explosion was small, and they had enough time to get off the boat before it went up.

Sitting with them in the St John Ambulance, listening to them repeat themselves again and again, 'We have lost everything', I had never seen my parents as vulnerable as I did in that moment. Words would not offer comfort, but there were actions I could take to ensure psychological first aid. As we sat there, I formulated a plan in my mind, how I could facilitate things that would make them feel safe and in control.

In good old North Yorkshire style, I bought my dad some beer, and my mum some chemist optical glasses so she could see what the hell was going on. My sisters, I bought a chocolate bar each. I organised them temporary housing and a few donations of clothes and essentials. All the while repeating that it was going to be okay, and taking the steps necessary until it actually was. And in the end? They got a better boat, and had quite the story to tell the other travellers on the canal.

So my key takeaway for you - whether the moment of reassurance is as small as someone not feeling good in an outfit, or something as traumatic as losing a home you should be 1) doing what you can to make them feel less alone 2) doing what you can to make them feel in control of their situation.

KALEY

When I started my 100 lunches journey, I felt I was the only person who suffered from social anxiety.

So I was surprised when many of the strangers told me they could relate to my struggles; it turned out other people felt uncomfortable in social situations and had insecurities - even really successful people.

One man I met was the chairman of a publicly listed company. When I showed up to our lunch, I brought a notepad so I could write down any business tips he passed on. He told me he was great at business - but terrible with women. He had a big fight with his girlfriend the day before and asked if I'd be willing to share some relationship advice. I gave him a few suggestions, and, the next day, to my delight, he told me he'd managed to win back his girlfriend by following my instructions.

I remember being surprised that somebody so successful could lack confidence. It taught me that even high achievers are human, and sometimes need reassurance. When I arrived at lunch with my notepad, I thought it would be him putting me at ease, so I was shocked when it ended up being me who put him at ease.

GANESH

Following the discussion with the lady I met over Teh C, I came out of the perplexed situation and decided to find avenues to help the needy. The pandemic had grappled with half of the world, and in April 2020 it looked like it was breaking into pieces with its healthcare complexities.

The Mayor of a small town in Italy, Mandello De Lario reached out to me for help as the city had reported maximum deaths and didn't have enough essentials to fight the deadly Coronavirus. The Mayor, Riccardo Fasoli, sent a message to me saying, 'We are experiencing something very similar to a war. The enemy is invisible, and it is amongst us. Many die alone, without having the chance to see family members.'

This shook me to the core and put me in an uneasy position. The feeling of helplessness annoys me and I thrive to find ways to help people and speak to the Almighty to help in testing times. Some divine energy did intervene, and I called the Mayor and told him that I will definitely help and to not lose hope.

I launched a fundraiser for Mandello which received an overwhelming response, and within a month we could send out help to the town. This experience I believe must have put the Mayor at ease, as the town was under tremendous pressure.

COEN

This is not really a situation with a stranger, but with someone I have only met once before, and we became Facebook friends. One day, he sent me a message out of the blue and said, 'Coen, I saw that you used to post your experiences about being in depression and having suicidal thoughts. Just the other day, I did the unthinkable, I started considering ways to commit suicide. I was wondering if I could talk to you.'

When I received that message, I was in the midst of something, so I quickly sent a message to him telling him we'd find time to talk as soon as I could. Later that evening, we spoke. I knew from my own experiences that in situations like that, the last thing he needed was advice, such as:

'You should be grateful! Think about all the people who didn't have what you had.'

That isn't helpful at all …

'You should think positive! Be happy!'

I would if I could help it! I actually feel that it's a form of tyranny to believe that people do not have the right to feel lousy.

And of course, here's possibly the worst thing to say …

'You should think about your loved ones, what would they do when you're gone?'

I recalled from my own experience that it made me feel even worse, that I had let my loved ones down, and that I was a disgrace to the family.

True enough, he shared that people around him were giving him all the above advice, but were not able to help him feel better. If anything, it drove him even deeper into despair.

Having been through that, I could empathize, so I said to him, 'Bro, I'm not here to tell you what to do, I'm just here to listen to you. So tell me about it ...'

And then I listened intently, and punctuated the conversation with questions, such as:

'What do you want? Why?'

'What's going on?'

'What is holding you back?'

'Why do you feel this way?'

And then I listened even more ...

His family had fallen on hard times financially, and so in order not to make the rest of his family worry unduly, he took out a loan from a loan shark in order to tide things over. Unfortunately, the loan amount ballooned, and he was at his wits end.

After allowing him to vent his emotions, I could hear him becoming calmer. But I still wanted to turn the tide of his emotions, so I took a risk and said this, 'Bro, I haven't known you very much to be frank ... But from what little I know about you, I know two things:

Firstly, you don't really want to die, do you? Because if you did, you would have done it! Telling people about it is a sign you don't want to do it, but what you really want is a little attention, someone who understands you, and perhaps some hope.

Secondly, it seems to me that you have a big heart to help other people around you. Unfortunately, when you overdo it, you unnecessarily take on too much for others, and they don't understand you, let alone appreciate you for it. Perhaps you feel the need to do so because you care, or because you're really looking to prove yourself. That's the 'rescuer complex' - you're trying to play the hero.'

I heard a deep, long exhale of breath over the phone...

'Yes Coen, you've nailed it! I've always felt like I am not good enough, so I realize that as a pattern in my life that I try to do too much, take on too much, just to prove myself. The truth is, I am afraid, and I feel hopeless. I don't know if I can take this anymore.'

Sensing I have made some headway, I pressed on.

'Now, the only thing you can do is to embrace this feeling that you really need help. You're trying so hard to be a hero for everyone, but even superheroes in the movies have downtime. They too need mentors, helpers. So it's late tonight, just go and have a good rest, but before that, write down on a piece of paper everything that you need help with. You're a successful salesperson, so you actually know how to make money. Making money is not the problem, giving up your ego and allowing others to help you is the real issue.'

I could hear that he was feeling a lot better, and more hopeful.

The next morning, I woke up to see a Facebook post he tagged me in.

is 😊 feeling grateful.
13 hrs · 👥
···

Just had an amazing conversation with a friend who helped open up my eyes and ears to my personality, understand myself and my strength and weaknesses.

We can't be everyone's hero, but everyone has a hero that is for them.

Thank you for being my hero tonight.

Coen Tan

👍 Like   💬 Comment   ↗ Share

Much as I was a 'hero' to him that night, it was also a transformational experience for me. It made me realize that little things I do can make a positive difference to someone else.

LYNDON

I was walking from Arre to Pamplona to meet Kerrie so we could celebrate our 25th wedding anniversary before I continued on. I was with an American couple, Nora and Guy - who were strangers only the night before - until we spent a few hours talking near the only clothes dryer in a monastery with over 100 pilgrims staying in it. It had rained that afternoon, so the dryer was in high demand.

As we passed through the impressive gates of Pamplona and discussed the awe we were feeling, we met another American lady with her son. He was looking and feeling very sick. She was stressing - when I say stressing she was visibly worried and upset. Explaining between anxious gasps that she needed to contact her husband at home, and the accommodation they would be late for that night because they had not walked as far as they wanted that day.

However, she did not have a sim card for her mobile and no stores were open. That is Spain on a Sunday - very little is open - except churches and bars. Nora and Guy had met her a few days earlier and were comforting her and making suggestions. I said I was going to the tourist office to use the Wi-Fi and she could use it to make a WhatsApp call.

A wave of realisation came over her and she relaxed, all the tension and stress fleeing her face only to be replaced with annoyance at herself saying, 'Why didn't I think of that.'

The five of us trudged and ambled - depending on our mood - to the tourist information center. When we arrived, I asked for Wi-Fi and called Kerrie. Our previously stressed friend conveyed her saga to the attendant who scolded her because, 'As a pilgrim you should know things in Spain are not open on Sunday.' I had never seen anyone so happy to be scolded.

CATHY

I had just moved to a new apartment - a house that had been converted into four separate rental units. I had only briefly met Sally and Joan, the neighbors around the corner - and then spent most of my time studying in my second year of MBA school.

I was working on a case study one Saturday afternoon when I heard Sally banging on my door yelling, 'We need your help! There's been an accident!' I jumped up and ran behind her not knowing what had happened, but knowing someone was in trouble. When I got to their place I saw Joan lying on the floor, with Sally beside her holding Joan's hand up in the air, and Joan was clearly distressed. I then learned that Joan had pulled one of the window sashes down to close it and had accidentally completely cut off the tip of one of her fingers in doing so. Sally asked me to come with her to the window Joan had closed and I saw the fingertip! That was unnerving!

I went back to Joan and sat beside her on the floor, grasping her hand and pressing the cloth to her finger. Joan was looking pale, and I decided to focus on keeping Joan's spirits up and her mind off what had happened to avoid something worse, like shock. I held her hand to the side, leaned in so she could see me, and began to make jokes about what happened. 'You wanted some attention, right? There are lots of ways to get attention, but noooo - you had to go and cut something off to make sure you got some big attention … ' Joan smiled and started to laugh. I kept going with whatever came to my mind, 'There's a doctor you're after, right? And you thought this would be a good way to get close to him, huh?' and she laughed even more.

I kept my impromptu comedy skit going and her color was coming back, but we knew we needed to get her to the hospital as soon as possible. I asked Sally to retrieve Joan's fingertip and put it on an ice cube in a paper cup, and then we drove to the emergency room. The whole way there my brain continued to come up with crazy humor that somehow worked for her. When we arrived at the hospital, the medical staff praised us for entertaining her and keeping her from going into shock - and for putting that fingertip on ice which meant they were able to sew it back on.

I forgot to ask about whether Joan and the doctor got together after that. Who knows?

MASAMI

On a B1G1 Study Tour 7 years ago, we were taking a group of business people from various countries to visit a school in Cambodia. We were there to help build a new playground so the kids there have access to a better learning environment and are encouraged to continue education.

There were high drop-out rates at every primary school in the region because local families wanted their kids to work. Sometimes, there were no choices. Feeding and taking care of younger siblings was commonly the responsibility of girls in those families.

It was a learning trip rather than a volunteering activity. We were all there to learn from local people and from the experience under the guidance of the local NGO, the school staff and local leaders.

When we arrived, the children at the school were initially very shy because they had never interacted with foreigners before. But after a little while, seeing us working clumsily and being covered in dirt and paint, they started to come closer with curiosity and started to help us. Many carried sand in buckets with great coordination. Some helped to paint the new swings we had just installed.

Soon, there was laughter everywhere. Hundreds of children were playing and working together with us. It felt like a great joyous day, although we were all working hard in direct sun and extreme heat.

At one point though, one of the teenage girls, the daughter of a businessman in our group, came to me and pointed to a little local girl who was crying in a corner of the playground. As we walked over, the little girl retreated, looking afraid.

Since we could not speak the local language, we went to fetch a teacher. I took this little girl's hand at first, then put her on my lap and asked the teacher to ask her what happened.

It turns out that her uniform was badly soiled with paint when she was painting the play equipment. She sobbed because she was convinced she would cause huge trouble for her parents who had no money to buy her a replacement uniform. Perhaps she was convinced she could not keep going to school if she didn't have the uniform.

You can probably imagine how bad we felt. After all, it was our fault that we didn't supervise the children well enough and protected their precious uniforms!

And at that moment, I saw myself in the little girl. I was that girl who was afraid, trying desperately not to trouble her parents.

I felt like I knew that girl. I squeezed her hand gently and said it was going to be all ok. There was nothing to worry about. Her sobs subsided eventually and she squeezed my hand back. Eventually, a smile was back on her face.

Luckily, the teenage girls and I were able to hop on a Tuk-Tuk to find a local market and buy multiple sets of uniforms to give to the teacher, so that if there were any other cases of damage, she could secretly distribute the replacement uniforms later.

I think what mattered the most that day was the feeling of connection we experienced among strangers. Often, words are not needed as much as the sharing of the feelings and experiences.

KERRIE

Coimbatore, India, March 2020. The hotel room next to ours had a sign outside, welcoming students for their IELTS (International English Language) exam. When I saw a young woman sit down in the foyer nearby, I asked her if she was here for the exam. She said, 'Yes,' and expressed her nervousness. We chatted for a little while about studying and working overseas, her hopes for the future, and my connections with international students in Australia. I encouraged her, saying, 'Your English is better than you think!'

It was only a few hours later that she messaged me to say that her results were higher than she expected, and that my encouragement meant the world to her, as she was able to let go of her anxiety and do well in the exam.

Just as I'd hoped! It only took a moment for a positive conversation, but according to her - it was a significant confidence booster.

SHARED ANXIETY
AND REASSURANCE

I posed an optional question about stories of shared anxiety, and shared reassurance. While I thought it was a relatively simple question, we found it challenging to answer. There must be so many times when we're in a dilemma or crisis with others and I think these situations can be forgotten, perhaps because of our relief that it's over, but it's worth unpacking some insights here. One of the key insights that has deepened over the past year is that we are at our best when serving others. When we are responsible for others, or feel that way, our attention turns from our own anxiety to a solution-focus. We might panic if we're on our own, but if we see that others need help, we tap into an inner strength to serve others, and often find shared tasks enjoyable because of the sense of community that grows.

Many of us are familiar with the cliche - 'we're all in the same boat'.

I've seen a meme spinning across the world online, 'we're not all in the same boat. We're all in the same storm.' As you consider your personal situation, in this storm called a pandemic, you might know of people who, by comparison, are in a very different boat. Some are safe and luxurious. Some are built for serving others. It's tough to be in those boats, and we're grateful for those who are serving. Some people are clinging to a scrap of wood to stay afloat.

Some people are clinging to life, and still have the capacity to selflessly reach out to others, working and hoping for the best together.

While some of these stories are about interactions with people we might consider strangers - those we didn't know before - we also can find a new depth of connection with someone we know well. Perhaps you've been in the company of friends, family and co-workers for years, and realise that in some ways they've become strangers to you - having new thoughts and ideas. We can deepen our relationships by asking new questions, and sharing new experiences together. If your intention is greater connection, you will find your conversations become more rewarding than ever.

ANNA

COVID-19 has highlighted to me the power of collective consciousness and care.

Let's go back to the Friday Cuddle group. Each week we tracked the themes and wellbeing scores of the people who participated. What was interesting was despite the groups being made up of people who had never spoken or even met, everyone said they felt isolated and said they felt anxious. In fact, everybody was feeling much of the same things. Week on week, the fluctuations in wellbeing scores were also reflective of changes happening in our broader political, social and economic environments.

As we live in our new 'COVID' reality, and as we have the wonderful benefit of hindsight over everything that's happened in 2020, we can see more than ever how connected everything in this world really is. This gives thought to how we impact others by our very existence and the way in which we conduct ourselves, in what we present to the world. Living is a balance between individual freedoms, self-reflection, the shared experience we have with those around us, and the comfort we take from that.

KALEY

I was particularly nervous when I arrived at the restaurant, because not only was Jodie the first woman I was going to meet on my 100 lunches journey, but also three other women had cancelled at the last moment. Was this about to happen for a fourth time? To my relief, Jodie didn't cancel. She was also incredibly warm and supportive, which meant a lot to me and helped me relax.

Funnily enough, months later, Jodie told me she had been thinking about cancelling at the last moment, because meeting a stranger felt so unnatural. Jodie was nervous too! However, I quickly put her at ease by smiling and being friendly.

So, without realising it, we found ourselves in a position of shared anxiety and shared reassurance. The power of kindness is amazing, isn't it?

CONOR

Three years ago, in April 2017, after choosing to leave my life as a Corporate Executive, Paula, my wife, and I had a shared anxiety of where life would take us.

By having 'conversations for our relationship', we found shared reassurance in a path forward.

Language creates new realities. By having conversations that we might feel are tough, it can enable a shared understanding to be created. In our case, these conversations enabled us to understand what was important to us and then move forward with a common purpose, both personally and professionally.

UNAMI

When I was pregnant with my third child, the doctors told us that she would need an operation as soon as she was delivered, which would be via caesarian section. Everything went according to plan and our daughter was born and had the operation, however things changed two weeks down the track. The baby was still in hospital as she still had to be fed through a tube and we were staying at the Ronald McDonald house with other families whose children were in hospital.

On Christmas of 2009, we received a phone call from the hospital and the nurse on the other end of the line said 'Your little girl is struggling to breathe.' My husband and I rushed to the hospital, two young children in tow with no idea what to expect. As we walked through the hospital doors of the paediatric intensive unit, all I could hear was the beeping of machines and the footsteps of doctors rushing through the waiting area.

They told my husband and I to step aside and I stood there in shock, feeling overwhelmed and unsure of what to do. I broke down in tears. I looked at my husband and he was not saying or shedding anything. I asked him 'How can you be so calm?' and his response was 'Well we can't both be crying'. In that moment it dawned on me that there was hope and knowing that there was someone else who was probably feeling what I was feeling and yet able to just 'hang in there', gave me the assurance that all was not lost and to hang in there myself.

NATHAN

It can happen in a split second. Sudden moments of shared anxiety often demand that someone take action to reassure others. Even when that same anxiety weighs on us.

While returning home from a weekend break at the coast with friends, we narrowly escaped a head on collision with a 42 tonne truck. The semi-trailer ploughed into an oncoming vehicle, throwing it into my lane; I swerved to avoid both the car and truck. The other car hit the curb, flying into the air, partially smashing through a wall, narrowly missing petrol pumps before coming to a stop, incredibly close to large gas tanks.

The wheels were still spinning, the engine still running.

Having just escaped an accident of our own, I ran to the scene, not knowing what to expect. Together with others on the scene we helped get the family out of the car, called emergency services and cleared the area. Fortunately, there were no major injuries or lives lost.

In a moment of shared anxiety, sometimes we look to others to take charge. Other times, people may look to us.

Helping others doesn't need to be dramatic. Regardless of how simple or complex the situation, it requires action from someone like you, to make a choice. The choice to turn around a moment of shared anxiety, by bringing hope and reassurance.

'Every time you smile at someone, it is an action of love, a gift to that person, a beautiful thing.'
Mother Teresa

COACHING CORNER

BEING HELPED

Can you think of a time when you were lost, confused, stressed or anxious and someone lifted your spirits?

How did it feel to be on the receiving end of support?

How do you feel about asking for help?

HELPING OTHERS

Can you describe a time when you realised your connection with someone decreased their anxiety or helped them out in a small or big way?

When did you smile, wave or connect with some kind of support, and witness another's relief?

When were you surprised by someone's gratitude for something that seemed very insignificant to you?

How did it feel to know that you helped someone?

PART 2

Building Confidence

BEING HELPED

Often all it takes is a word, a smile or a conversation to boost your confidence.

We hear so many stories of how a mere word or gesture has sparked a boost in confidence, for all kinds of moments or choices. People share examples, such as a career choice, more confidently made after chatting with someone in a shared waiting room, or a choice to do a bungy jump, skydive or get on a bike for the first time in a long time - or ever! In Connect With Confidence workshops, presentations and online events - besides all the everyday interactions with people - I never tire of hearing about these moments, because they all matter. And the joy in someone's face as they acknowledge their brave moments, boosted by the influence of a stranger - sometimes it seems that the stranger is celebrated as much as the courageous steps. Remember the times you were more confident or assured because of the support of others? Perhaps your boost in confidence was not for a specific task, or related to your skills, but simply, and most importantly, it grew your confidence in who you are, and in how you show up in the world. It said that YOU MATTER.

I asked my friends to share a time when their confidence grew because of the kindness of a stranger.

NATHAN

They say it takes a village to raise a child. Sometimes it takes a circus. Or both.

People often struggle with kindness because they're unsure of how it should look or feel. Should it be a home cooked meal with a greeting card? A trip to the circus? For each of us, kindness is packaged differently.

While I was sitting in the school library as a 12 year old boy, reading a book alone, my brother was lying in an intensive care unit bed. A cyclone-grade wind storm had ripped through our home town, and my brother was caught in an accident, inflicting traumatic brain injury and many broken bones. He died twice, yet somehow lived.

It was an extremely difficult time for our family.

Surviving reconstructive surgery and enduring a long recovery, he went on to become the incredible person he is today. But we didn't know the outcome then. All we knew was uncertainty.

For a long time he was in a Sydney hospital with our parents far from home, and our extended family looked after my sister and me. Friends kindly supported us with home cooked meals, often accompanied with an encouraging card. Exactly what we needed.

During a particularly difficult week, we received an invitation. Our school librarian invited my sister and I to go to the circus. A trip to the circus to watch animals do tricks? When our brother may not live? It felt irreverent, but a distraction was what we needed most.

This memory stands out because, although the librarian barely knew us, she knew what kindness looked like. An invitation. That night offered temporary relief that transported us above life's difficulties, helping us face the coming days.

That's what kindness looks like to me.

ANUPAMA

In May 2019, I was getting ready to host a gala night at a conference, and I was all dressed up, looking my best, sparkles in my ears and stars in my eyes at the prospect of the evening that lay ahead. But I was a bit nervous too, because earlier in the day, I had a couple of strangers make some judgemental comments when I mentioned I would be hosting the gala night.

Though I was a bit anxious, I tried to tell myself that it was nothing, because they were probably judging me on my 'current' appearance. Actually, I looked like a nerd in my black rimmed reading glasses, black cardigan, faded jeans and boots. Surely, they were not able to imagine that a petite, studious-looking girl would transform into a glamorous one in the evening. But I was anxious, also because I knew I would be on stage in front of 200 professional speakers and I am new to the industry.

It was nearly show-time. I reached backstage and stood for a moment in the shadows. I saw someone coming towards me with the microphone that I needed to be hooked up with. She was a young girl, possibly 25 years younger than me. As she reached me, her eyes widened and she mouthed the words - 'WOW, You look so HOT!'.

As I was still processing this and suddenly feeling a warm glow spreading inside of me - thanks to that simple compliment from someone I was meeting for the first time - I felt my nervousness fall away.

The next minute, the sound manager asked me to step onto the stage for a sound check - 'Give it your all' he said. And I did! Looking sideways at the girl encouraging from the shadows, I saw her pointing to the back of the room where about a dozen men who had been setting up tables and arranging cutlery had stopped what they were doing and were staring at me!

I am so glad she was there that day, a person who had seen me for the first time, who was from another culture and background, and with a kind gesture and some supportive words, she helped me step onto the stage, literally and figuratively, with confidence.

JULIE

Not long after I went blind I began speaking to donors of Blind Low Vision NZ. The first time I spoke I was scared to death, but people seemed to like hearing my story so I said, 'Why not' again, this time travelling to a south island town in New Zealand called Timaru. After I had spoken, a man came up to me to shake my hand. He didn't let go and said, 'Thank you, Julie, for coming today. You see I'm going blind and before I heard you today, I was scared, but after listening to your story, I'm no longer frightened.' I felt ten feet tall. This total stranger had affirmed my decision to speak and gave me the confidence to do it again, knowing I had made a difference to the life of one blind man.

CONOR

In August 1999 I was a week into a new role as the Logistics Director of a drinks wholesale business in the UK and I had to announce, on-site and in person, the closure of a distribution depot, as part of a major supply chain restructuring.

It was the first time I had ever been out of the third-party logistics sector in my 10-year career. I was brought into the leadership team of the business to execute a transformational logistics strategy. I was confident but anxious.

After announcing the closure of the site in person to those affected, one of the drivers came up to me and said, 'I saw an announcement that you only joined the Company last week, this must have been a really challenging thing for you to do. Thank you for doing it in person.' This, coming from someone who had just been told that he had lost his job, was true kindness and without a doubt gave me the confidence thereafter to do the job I was employed to do.

How we legitimise the other person we are having a conversation with by understanding their stories and where they are 'coming from' is crucial to our ability to see the humanity in front of us. In this case, not simply a cost to be saved on the Profit & Loss or balance sheet. In my Coaching Practice, I label this, 'the legitimate other'.

KATIE

In 2019, after we hiked El Camino de Santiago, we made our way to Sweden to hike St. Olav's Way, another pilgrimage. This hike was much wilder, a lot of backcountry and much fewer accommodations. Many times we had to stop along the trail to ask for help from strangers - to fill our water jug, to set up our tent in a clearing on their property. Asking for help is hard enough, but then accepting such overwhelming generosity is sometimes even harder. Nine times out of ten, we were received warmly and given even more than we asked for.

One of our most treasured memories is when we stopped to ask for our water bottles to be filled. They invited us to sit on the porch and took our bottles and disappeared to fill them up. When the woman of the house returned with the bottles filled, the man of the house came back with a couple of cold beers. We gladly accepted and toasted to new friends.

Then a second round of beers came out. Andy gestured at the tables set up in the front yard and commented that it looked like they were getting ready to have a party. Torgny, the man of the house, said yes, they were having their annual end of summer celebration for the village.

He said something in Swedish to his partner, Ulrika, and then turned to us and said, 'Do you want to stay for dinner?'

We had been eating a lot of instant noodles and trail mix, so a home-cooked meal sounded like a dream come true. We gladly accepted the invitation. Then they showed us where the showers were so that we could clean up before dinner (a benefit for everyone, as it had been a few days since our last shower). We couldn't believe our luck.

When the rest of the village arrived (two other families), our hosts explained who we were. They were so delighted and wanted to hear about our travels and how we ended up there. We ate, drank, and visited for hours. We stayed so late into the night that our hosts let us sleep in their guest room. Then they so kindly made us breakfast the next morning before we set out on the trail.

This was just the first of several interactions that were so incredibly gracious and kind and went above and beyond our expectations. If you can work up the courage to ask a stranger for help, you better be prepared to receive some blessings!

SIMON

Two moments immediately come to mind.

I was about 15 years old and at this point in my life, I was quite shy, dorky and awkward. I was a creative person in the traditional sense, and yet I hadn't really shown anyone my art before. I was yet to kiss a girl, and yet to do anything particularly exciting in life.

Slowly but surely this started to change, which was partially due to two incredibly important books. The first was a book called Yes Man by Danny Wallace and the second embarrassingly enough was a book by Neil Strauss, called The Rules of the Game.

Yes Man was all about saying yes to life and The Rules of the Game was an instruction manual about how to talk to and 'pick up' women. These two books converged at the same time, and I soon found myself taking risks and putting myself out there more ... gradually.

One day at school I found the courage to hold my arms open and gesture to the girl I had a crush on to give me a hug - something I would never have done before out of fear of rejection or ridicule. In my mind, she saw me as a platonic friend and nothing more, and so I was simply waiting for that awkward moment where she tells me to put down my arms. Instead, she came running and reciprocated my gesture. My world opened up at that point, my doubts, fears and imaginary hurdles faded away. She had absolutely no idea how much it meant to me and how big an influence it had on me.

The other instance was following some advice in The Rules of the Game, which was simply to build up more confidence. It said; 'Operation Small Talk. Make small talk with five strangers today.'

That day I was on a trip to an amusement park, so I knew I would have a chance to practice this in all of the various queues.

Annoyingly, my nerves got the better of me throughout the day and I wussed out, keeping my head down and avoiding eye contact.

On the final ride of the day, in the final stretch of the queue, I summoned all of my strength and plucked up the courage to tell the chap in front of me that I liked his glasses. I'm pretty sure I sounded like a madman as I basically shouted it and he was turning away from me. Fortunately, I think he took pity on me, said, 'Thank you.' and turned back around.

As we shuffled forward, he turned to me again, and we proceeded to chat about the perils of wearing glasses on fast rides. It was a truly innocuous discussion, but one that meant a lot to me. All day, I'd completely forgotten my fear of heights and had instead been sweating, worrying and stressing myself out over the conversation task. All, it seems, for nothing.

Strangers aren't scary, they're mostly lovely, and this chap has no idea how much that conversation meant to me, and how big an effect it had on my confidence. Upon reflection, I wouldn't be doing what I'm doing now had I not accepted the challenge and taken that initial risk.

UNAMI

In August 2019 I was on a flight from America back to Australia after attending a conference. The lady I was sitting next to offered me her aisle seat. She said to me that, since I was tall and it was a long flight,

I would most likely benefit from having the extra legroom than she would. She expressed that because she was shorter than me, she did not need her allocated seat. I was surprised and confused at the same time, and there was a part of me that was sceptical and was expecting something else to come up.

I was not used to that level of kindness from a stranger. I felt really good afterwards as I reflected on the fact that contrary to other experiences I had been through in the past, there truly are still some kind souls out there. This experience challenged me to pay it forward and be more intentional in my interactions with other people as I felt emboldened to be kind myself.

SERENE

I was a new mother in a Facebook group for parents. I'd had a rocky start to motherhood and I felt truly inadequate. I had postnatal blues, and it was always in the dead of night, when I got up to feed my baby, that it all became very overwhelming. But then I found that when I would share my issues in the group, someone, usually also a new mother breastfeeding her child at night, would reply that they went through the same thing. And many a time, they would say, 'you're doing good'. Whether or not it was true, it made me feel like I could do it too. That I wasn't the terrible mother I'd feared I was. That I could actually be a decent mother if I tried my best.

Motherhood is in my opinion the most guilt-inducing endeavor you could ever do in your life. Nothing I did ever felt good enough. I constantly worried that I was ruining my kid's life. It wasn't true of course, but in the neverending drudgery of day to day caregiving, it was easy to see the myriad mistakes I was making every moment. So when someone else told me, I'm a good mother, or that I was right in making a certain decision, I felt validated. And even that meagre validation was enough to stave off the feelings of incompetence and let me carry on for this moment.

ANNA

I've spent years in the social impact sector. Bambuddha Group has had multiple lives, and it has taken the input and contribution from a lot of people to get where we are today. One stranger came along at the start of 2020, someone with a similar vision for reducing inequalities and who was working in the same space. She scheduled a meeting with me and we quickly found that we had completely complementary skill sets, a shared sense of humour and that together, we could create the scalable model needed to accelerate our impact. In that first interaction we could see each other so clearly. Her belief in our vision and how she took the time to understand where we needed help and how we could best be supported brought a tear to my eye. I didn't realise how much that interaction would change my life. But that stranger is now our Bambuddha Programs Director who continues to take our coaching solutions and research to the next level.

PATRICK

Nine months after I self-published my book The Connector's Way: A Story About Building Business One Relationship at a Time, I had only sold a couple of hundred copies, and thought that it would never take off. I gave away five copies of the book to people who I interviewed in preparation to speak at their company's annual sales event. One of the recipients liked the book so much that she used it to craft her annual sales plan. She then gifted a copy of my book to her mentor, who was a highly successful business coach. She included a note encouraging him to read the book since it has made such a positive impact on her thinking.

A few weeks later, her mentor called me to let me know how much he enjoyed the book. At the time, I had no idea who he was or what difference his enthusiasm would make. Then, a couple of days later, he went on his weekly YouTube broadcast and encouraged his followers to buy my book and read it carefully. Immediately, book sales started to grow. The coach invited me to deliver the keynote speech at his company's big annual conference. The day before my important presentation, the woman who had given the book to the coach walked me around the kickoff reception introducing me to her friends. I was surprised and delighted with how many people had read and enjoyed my book. I signed a lot of autographs and had many requests for 'selfies'. Meeting so many enthusiastic readers who were going to be in my audience the next day boosted my confidence and enthusiasm. I channeled these positive feelings into my keynote presentation, which led to even greater book sales and invitations to speak to companies around the country. I am still getting new business from people in that audience!

I remind myself of this story whenever I am feeling down. The lesson I've drawn is that I will never know who will give me my next great business referral - or when it will come. All I can do is give my knowledge enthusiastically and have faith that good things will happen in due time.

KALEY

My confidence grew not because of the kindness of just one stranger, but because of the kindness of the 100 strangers I lunched with during 2018.

My initial lunches were so nerve-wracking, they almost felt like a punishment. But after the first 10 or so lunches, I began to feel a lot more comfortable.

Why? Because the strangers I'd met had been so warm and supportive. They'd drawn me out of my shell and helped me become a better conversationalist. Now, instead of mumbling the odd word here and there, I was telling interesting stories, asking thoughtful questions and steering conversations.

As the lunches continued, my growth continued - again, thanks in large part to the wonderful strangers I was meeting. About halfway through that 100 lunches journey, I stopped thinking of myself as socially awkward and started thinking of myself as a good communicator. My identity had changed.

I also became increasingly confident. By confident, I don't mean I thought I was better than anyone - that's arrogance, not confidence. Instead, I realised I could just be me, without needing to compare myself to anyone else.

When my lunches started, I thought of myself as an outsider, because I was an immigrant who could never fit the mould of a 'typical Aussie'. But as I met more and more people, I realised there is no mould, because we're all unique. All the Anglo-Australians I met were unique in some way; and many of the people I met actually weren't Anglo, because Melbourne is such a multicultural place.

That gave me the confidence to be me. Now, when I meet a stranger or go into a business meeting, I don't compare myself to others. Why would I? I'm unique and so are they.

I never would've become the confident woman I am today without the incredible support of all those strangers I had lunch with.

GANESH

I was travelling alone from London to Edinburgh on a LNER train which was a 5 hour 20 minute journey. The city was new to me and so was the experience as it was the first time I was visiting a place without even booking a hotel.

A few hours into the journey and I was becoming more nervous as the fear of the unknown continued creeping in.

Just before Durham station an older couple stepped onto the train and sat opposite me. After settling down, they looked at me and asked me why I was worried.

Before I could answer her question she told me that the train crossed a viaduct giving superb views of Durham city, castle & cathedral on the right-hand side. She involved me in understanding the culture and ethos of the city and asked me about my itinerary.

When I told her about my trip, she encouraged me to carry no fear whatsoever as Edinburgh is a warm and friendly city for the tourist traveling alone. She also explained to me about the exotic food the city offered and detailed the signature tourist spots I should visit.

The couple left the train after a few stops, and we exchanged lovely smiles when we parted ways. I was so moved by their generosity that I didn't even think to take their contact details. After reaching Edinburgh I followed the instructions the old lady gave and ate the food she suggested. As I reflected on the experience later, I felt it was a unique experience. They only expressed interest in me and shared about the city, but didn't make it about themselves at all. There was no business motive, nothing they wanted in return from me. It was all about giving wholeheartedly.

Overall, I embraced my time in the castle city and thanked the old couple in my spirit for teaching me a lesson of 'living with no fear of the unknown'.

Sometimes, I think the couple got onto the train as my guiding spirits as they moved me from my negative feelings to enjoying the present.

If you treat strangers with compassion and trust them, they will surely add value to your life.

CATHY

About 8 years ago, I was asked to facilitate my first workshop in Japan. It was for a global bank, and although I had done that workshop for the company in Singapore, Shanghai and Hong Kong, I had never done it for a Japanese audience. I arrived at the company's Tokyo office early in the morning and found the room where the workshop was to be held. As I was setting up, I remember wondering what this day would be like and feeling a bit unsure about how this group would respond to me and to the learning.

And then it happened. As people began coming in and finding their seats, a young man said to me with a slight bow, 'You must be Cathy Johnson. I've heard you're a great teacher.' What a welcome! He then shared that he had heard that from three other colleagues in the company so he was really looking forward to the day. I hadn't been exactly worried before, but his comment definitely buoyed my confidence and helped me to step into the program with even greater poise. And it went really well.

COEN

In November 2014, I was speaking on a cruise ship for the first time as a cruise enrichment lecturer. As part of the entertainment program for the cruise passengers, the speeches had to be interesting, not 'corporate like' and had to have general appeal. So I elected to speak about relationships, using what I know about personality types and how they might be interesting information.

However, when I showed up on the ship, I looked all around me and realized I was probably the youngest person on the ship who wasn't a crew member. All around me were people in their 60s, 70s and 80s. At the buffet area the first night, I thought I would go around to make friends and get to know some people in case they would turn out at my lecture. They told me stories about their 50+ years of marriage and showed me pictures of their grandchildren.

You can excuse me for feeling a serious bout of impostor syndrome there and then…

There I was, an Asian man in my mid-thirties, single and ready to mingle, never been married before, and I was supposed to be lecturing about relationships to these people who could be my parents or even grandparents!

During my first lecture, I was so nervous that I fumbled my lines badly. Unlike a corporate audience, these people had no qualms about leaving. Halfway through my talk, 90% of the people had already left! I was so demoralized after that.

But where was I to go?

The ship had left port on a 19-day journey from Singapore to Australia.

The only way I could leave was to jump overboard, or disembark on the next port and pay my own flight home, and break the agreement I signed with the cruise company. There was simply nowhere I could go. I had signed on to give 12 speeches and I had another 11 lectures in the coming days.

On the next talk, I was alarmed to find that there were less than ten people in attendance. In the cavernous theatre that would seat at least 1,500, it was a very cold and empty room indeed.

However, it gave me an opportunity to pay attention to who showed up. There was an elderly Aussie couple who showed up for every single one of my lectures, and they would sit right up front. When I shared with them how demoralized I felt after the first lecture, and so discouraged I felt when the turnout was so low, she gave me a hug and said, 'Don't worry about it son! You can only just do the best you can. We all do!'

That made me feel so good and gave me the courage to continue delivering. In the subsequent days of the trip, we'd hang out together at the bars and restaurants, chatting. We became such close friends that in 2016, she invited my wife and I to go visit her in her beautiful home by the ocean in New South Wales, Australia. It was a 3 hour drive from Sydney, and was one of the most peaceful, beautiful beach areas we've ever been to. We spent a full week at her place, with accommodation, food and day trips all taken care of. We had a great time and my wife and I often reflect on this experience.

Unfortunately, she recently passed on at the age of 88 years old. We reached out to her family, but they did not inform us why she had passed away. Our countries' borders are closed because of the COVID-19 pandemic, which was a pity because we'd have flown over to Australia to pay our last respects.

She'll be remembered as one of the kindest people I've ever known.

MASAMI

I always had trouble speaking in front of others.

That started from my earliest memory of being in a class at school in Japan.

As a quiet, shy girl, I already had challenges talking in front of others. My father - a dedicated, hardworking businessman in Japan - was periodically transferred to different cities by his company. And when that happened, I moved to a new school in the middle of a semester.

I didn't know how to make friends and blend into a very new environment where kids spoke and behaved differently. With that fear of rejection, I developed the habit of becoming totally silent or crying uncontrollably whenever I was asked to express my thoughts.

But years later, I started to speak at business events simply out of necessity. You probably could imagine how scary it was for me to deliver a public speech, even to a very small group. I even had the additional language barrier to overcome.

Luckily, I surrendered. And even though my speeches were never perfect or sophisticated, there were people who came over to me afterwards to give me words of encouragement. And that encouragement from strangers kept me going.

Without that, I might have given up long ago.

So, thank you... for also being the one to encourage others who are doing their best in a time of utmost vulnerability.

KERRIE

We often have no idea if we've made a difference, or done something well - and it's so helpful to know, because otherwise we might give up and assume it doesn't matter.

The first time I spoke to a crowd of 1000 people, they were in a very long, darkened stadium, in Manila, and I could only hope from the brightly lit stage, that it was engaging for everyone throughout what seemed to be jam-packed seating.

The energy at the front of the room was amazing, but I really was literally 'in the dark' about the experience at the back.

After dinner with a team of 20 business leaders, I was leaving the restaurant and one of the leaders stepped up to say that she had spent part of my presentation in the back row, and part of it in the front row. She wanted me to know that it was just as exciting and engaging from the back of the stadium to the front.

I think that says something of her enthusiasm, and her kindness, in passing that on to me, but it was also a relief and encouragement to me that I could speak to a large crowd and have an impact on individuals anywhere. Wherever people are - as long as the audio works well - I can reach them and encourage them - especially if they come with open hearts and minds as these beautiful people did.

HELPING OTHERS

And then there's the times you boosted someone's confidence, maybe intentionally, seeing they could benefit from a smile - and sometimes your moment of kind attention was a greater gift than you imagined.

So I asked my friends: when have you greeted someone and discovered your connection meant more to them than you'd guess?

When did your genuine smile mean more than you thought it would?

CONOR

In July 2006, as a new executive in Australia, I was told that the way I greeted a senior leader in my first meeting with him, and what I asked him, made a lasting impression on him of how leaders should lead.

In that meeting, I simply asked him about himself and his family first, and then about his role and what his key objectives and challenges were.

As an MD today, he told me recently that 'the talent and leadership in that business was incredibly strong, and I put you right at the very top of that. It certainly helped shape me into the leader I am today'.

It felt natural to put the person before the job. Maybe that is something we should all do more of, even at times of extreme pressure, when we might only be focused on the task or outcome?

LYNDON

Back to the Camino. I was walking with Alfie, a British/American pilgrim I had met in Estrella several days before where he asked for directions to the Camino. We met again a few days later and stayed at the same Alburge that night. In the morning I offered to walk with him because his feet were badly blistered. Alfie normally walked fast to catch up with strangers he would make friends with, but was unable to this day because of the pain.

As we were finding our way out of Logroño, we crossed a busy road and passed an old lady who schlepped across the road, looking like she was in more pain than my fellow pilgrim. She was hunched over a walker and stepping very gingerly.

I leant over and looked into her face, smiled and said, '¡Buenos días!'

She stopped right there in the middle of the road, raising her head to look at me with what appeared to be confusion and disbelief that anyone from the throng of people passing had spoken to her - no my Spanish is not so bad that she didn't understand me.

So, smiling, I repeated, '¡Buenos días!'

Her dull eyes went bright and shiny as a wide smile cracked into a canyon on her face, distinguishing it from the deep wrinkles. 'Gracias, gracias, buenos días. ¡Sí, buenos días!,' was her jubilant reply.

Alfie and I kept on walking, leaving her to stand in the middle of the road. When I looked back, I would swear she was standing taller and with her schlepp left in the gutter was walking faster, her face beaming like a traffic light.

I realised that a simple hello can mean so much more than simply just a greeting. It can mean the difference between someone feeling alone in a crowd or acknowledged and seen as a human being, another pilgrim on this journey we call life.

JULIE

I was in India in a hotel with my husband Ron. It was a big hotel, and we kept getting lost, but thanks to the lovely young porter Nhidi Pandey, we managed to make our way back to our hotel room. I decided I would write Nhidi Pandey's name in braille and present it to her the following morning upon checking out. I said to her when she came to our room, 'I have a little gift for you', handing it to her. As I explained what it was, she cried, saying 'words cannot express how I am feeling at this time.'

This moment changed my life, as it was a moment I referred back to in 2017 when I turned 20 years blind and decided to set myself a goal of writing 1 million names in braille, thanks to Nhidi Pandey's response to my little act of kindness.

KATIE

About two weeks into Camino de Santiago, our pilgrimage across Spain, we were introduced to Nicole, a fellow pilgrim who was from a city only a few hours away from our hometown back in the US. She was practically our neighbor!

She was exhausted from trying to keep pace with the pilgrims she had started the Camino with, and it was interfering with her spiritual journey as well (her walking companions were not walking for religious reasons, as she was).

Our companion who introduced us encouraged her to join our merry band. I could see the concern on her face - she didn't want to abandon her other friends, she didn't want to slow her pace, but she was in pain and she didn't want to walk alone. I knew she was conflicted. I encouraged her to join up with us, even if it was only for a little while. I promised that we would get an early start the next day and offered to carry some of her extra pack weight. She declined the offer, but seemed grateful to have company for a slower, more sustainable pace.

As we walked together, we were able to chat and get to know each other. We exchanged stories about college, travels, and relationships. Day by day, we laughed and joked and sang and danced our way along the trail.

After several days of walking together, Nicole told me she was recovering from an unhealthy, abusive relationship. She said it was such a blessing to see me and my husband's love for each other and the way we cared for each other, even on the most challenging days on the trail.

I was so touched by her sharing this story and so grateful that she accepted our invitation to walk with us. We spent the next 30 days walking together. When we finally parted ways to continue on our own journeys, it was a tearful goodbye. A friendship of a lifetime developed from that first smile and, 'Hey, walk with us!'

SIMON

It was quite early on in the days of Professional Weirdos and I'd managed to secure a speaking gig at the head offices of a well-known company in the UK called John Lewis. Quite a large crowd had turned up and I was nervous.

The subject matter of what I talk about through Professional Weirdos can be somewhat divisive, so naturally, in the early days at least, I noticed mixed reactions to varying degrees.

Some people took to it immediately and nodded along throughout, whilst others turned off almost straight away.

I started my talk with the typical vigour I bring to all of my sessions and started to see the same patterns emerge. Some people were laughing, enjoying and nodding along, whilst others were slightly glazed over.

I finished the talk and was met with the classically British polite round of applause. A smattering of people came up to chat with me at the end; the part of the session I enjoy the most and I subsequently left the offices feeling as though it had been a job well done and that if nothing else, the experience would be something great to put on the resume.

A few days later, however, I got a notification on Linkedin. It was from a lovely girl called Zoe. She had taken time out of her busy day to write me a long thank you message for the talk. She went on to explain that she'd often felt out of place in the world and that she resonated with a lot of what I talked about in my session and that it had made her feel more confident and brought a smile to her face throughout. She said that she was quite a shy person but felt so connected that she wanted to reach out.

I was blown away by the message - it impacted me greatly and deeply humbled me. It reminded me of the importance and joy of connecting with people as individuals, and not just as a faceless group of people.

Now I realise that we both made a bigger impact on one another than we knew.

CATHY

About four years ago, I was one of the organizers and emcees for the annual Speakers Academy for Asia Professional Speakers Singapore association (APSS). Actually mostly I was a sidekick for the real Organizer and Emcee, Tim Wade, but I was there early helping to set up in the newest and biggest space we had ever held Speakers Academy in.

At 9:00 am the room was full and we began. After Tim and I introduced ourselves and welcomed everyone, I got off the stage to continue to do the behind the scenes work which included greeting people and getting them seated. I noticed there was a woman who I'd never seen before at an APSS event, and she looked like she didn't know anyone - she looked lost. So I walked up to her and said, 'Welcome! It's so great to see you here!' - and I hugged her.

I'm a hugger - all my family is - and although I know not everyone is comfortable with hugging, I had the sense that this woman was ok about it, and she was. She hugged me back, a real hug, and seemed both surprised and very happy to be welcomed so heartily. She had a huge smile on her face and she told me she had been so nervous coming to our Speakers Academy since she knew no one at all here, but my warm welcome made her feel so welcomed and a part of the event already.

I introduced her to several people so she made some new friends early on, and every time I saw her those two days, she was always with someone and smiling. But what I didn't know was how much my welcome and hug had impacted her. To this day, whenever I see her she reminds me of that time at Speakers Academy when I made her feel like she belonged there, and like she was somebody - like she really mattered. And she does.

UNAMI

Whenever I meet new people, I make a conscious effort to remember their name and some other personal detail about them. When I make a connection with someone to the point that we exchange phone numbers I will often save their name and extra personal details under their name in my phone. For example, someone might tell me that they like going fishing on weekends, I would save that detail so that when I speak to them next, I can make reference to that detail and this usually gets a smile from people as they are surprised that I remember that information but also that I am interested enough to want to know more about them by speaking about something they may have told me in passing.

SERENE

We were part of the same classical book club on Facebook. This Pakistani man, almost half my age, a computer engineer who had never left his hometown, and me, a Singapore mother and international speaker. I saw him comment repeatedly, so I sometimes replied. We became Facebook friends, and I used to say 'Hello' whenever I saw him online.

As time went by, we got closer, and I realised that I was his first female friend, that he used to be a shy, depressed young man who had real issues connecting to women and forming relationships. And that the simple greetings and comments we started with were his first step towards forming his own connections, making friends, going to other countries for work, taking up dancing and gym, and searching for his own life partner.

I won't dare take credit for all the work he's done. He has transformed himself, and he has truly worked hard over the years to do it. But it still makes me happy that those simple hellos were his first step.

ANUPAMA

As I stepped out of the lift in my office building and moved towards the entrance, I was glad I had a big umbrella. It was raining cats and dogs! I also felt my heart start singing as the fragrant breeze carrying light droplets of water played with my hair. As I stopped to open the umbrella, I saw a lady in red standing in the lobby, looking very anxious and fidgeting. I started thinking, She doesn't have an umbrella … She needs to get to a meeting … She is not able to book a taxi … Her phone battery has run out…

I could not have charged her phone but could have helped her book a taxi or call someone, so I asked her, 'Hey! Are you doing ok - can I help you in any way?'

She looked up and turned to me - just staring at me with her big, gorgeous eyes - suddenly full of hope and longing to ask me for something. But, I think, also not knowing what to say to me. So I prodded on, 'Can I walk you to the MRT station? It is just 5 minutes away, and this umbrella is big enough to save both of us getting drenched in the rain!'

She had been so tense I think that all she could say was, 'Oh - thank you! Would you mind?'

'Not at all! Would love to walk in the rain with someone', I said as we stepped out. I started humming a famous Hindi romantic rain song - she was also Indian. 'Ek Chatri aur hum hai do, ab kya ho, kuch to karo … bheegne do, zaraa, bheegne do'. Translation: We have one umbrella and we are two, what to do now? Please do something... let's get wet in the rain, a little, let's get wet in the rain'.

She burst into a lilting laugh and we hopped over puddles of water together, laughing and chatting, and she told me that I had such a kind and generous heart to help a stranger like this. I just smiled and told her it was the least I could have done to help a stranded woman! We were nearing the metro station by now and exchanged names and said our goodbyes!

A few days later, I was pleasantly surprised as she reached out on LinkedIn and offered to treat me to a coffee so she could thank me properly. We met up and before we realized it, we were telling each other our life stories. She told me how she had been working/traveling to Singapore for the last ten years and had only professional contacts here - not many close friends as she was always on the move. We met up three times that week - it was almost as if the Universe had designed the heavy rain shower so we could meet. Interestingly, her name also means 'Rain'.

A few months later, we have become the best of friends, inspiring each other to make progress in areas we are good at. She offered to get the website made for my first book and she is also helping me with digital work for two of my companies. She says she found in me a friend and a pillar of positivity and inspiration which inspires her to new vistas of growth.

A chance meeting, an offer to help, a follow up with a stranger and both of us received from each other, something we needed in our lives. How wonderful is that for building good karma with simple acts of kindness?

ANNA

When I became a keynote speaker the biggest challenge was to expose the real me. I have always been a storyteller. However until then, my job, whether in marketing or partnerships, had been telling other brand's and people's stories. I never realised how hard I would find it to tell my story. The first few times I was physically sick and wracked with nerves. Talking so honestly meant I was reliving so many experiences and feelings, and I felt I had no control over my response to them.

What is interesting is who comes up to speak to you after each gig. Often, the most unlikely candidates come up and tell me that they feel so much less alone. Just by talking, you relieve the pressure that people put on themselves. So many friends over the years have told me that I help them feel less alone and more connected. I think it's because I appreciate the feeling of seeing someone and being seen in return. A 'meet cute' is one of my favorite things. In a split second you explore the boundaries of how you can communicate, agreeing without saying that, 'Yep, we're each other's cup of tea.'

PATRICK

I was on a late-night flight and completely exhausted due to an eight-hour flight delay. I could not wait to get onto the plane and fall asleep. When I saw that I was seated next to a five or six-year-old boy and his frazzled mother, I was not happy. 'There goes my chance to get some rest,' I said to myself.

The boy was full of energy. He fiddled with the built-in screen in the seat in front of him, trying unsuccessfully to make it work. When I offered to help, he didn't understand me. Since I noticed that he and his mother were speaking to each other in Spanish, I told him in Spanish that I could fix the screen. His face lit up when he discovered that we could communicate. During our three-hour flight, the boy and I talked about his favorite cartoons and games. His mother shared that they were fleeing Honduras due to violent acts that she and her family had experienced. The conversation then pivoted to the work she planned to do in the United States, and I was relieved to learn that she was going to be reunited with family members when our plane arrived.

During our conversation, the mother told me she was surprised an American would take the time to learn Spanish. I told her how much I enjoyed speaking Spanish because there are so many Spanish speakers in the United States. The mother told me she was nervous about not speaking English well, and I reassured her that she would learn since she was motivated and smart.

When we were exiting the plane, the mother thanked me for treating her and her son with kindness and making them feel welcome. She told me that our conversation was especially meaningful since many of her Honduran friends had told her that Americans weren't friendly to immigrants.

Interacting with the Honduran mother and her son reminded me of important things that we can easily forget in the frenzy of daily living. We all have the capacity to make a big difference in people's lives with simple, thoughtful words and actions. And, in helping others, we give our lives a greater sense of meaning and joy.

KALEY

Nowadays, as a keynote speaker, I'm in the privileged position of regularly being able to impact people's lives, with acts that seem small to me but end up meaning more to others than I realised in the moment.

Years ago, I was a shy immigrant woman who was crippled by anxiety, low on confidence and achieving far less than her potential. But having lunch with 100 strangers in 2018 helped me overcome those problems. I've discovered that when I share my story with others - especially the really personal and even humiliating parts - I'm able to build emotional connections with complete strangers and help them achieve significant personal growth.

To take one typical example, I remember giving a speech to a room full of high school students. One girl, who was probably 17 or 18, mustered the courage to approach me. I smiled and responded with very positive body language. She was really nervous, because talking to a stranger was way outside her comfort zone. But my friendly reaction soothed her. Within a minute, I noticed the tension drain from her body. She calmed down, started smiling and looked more assured. It was like I was speaking to a different person. She told me I had given her the confidence to engage with strangers and that she planned to embark on her own 100 lunches journey.

For me, this was just another encounter; for that lovely girl, it might've been a life-changing event. Not because I'm anything special, but because I gave her permission to be herself and encouraged her to aim high - much like all those strangers I'd met on my 100 lunches journey had done for me.

GANESH

There are many strangers around us, and a recent memorable experience I had was with a toddler. The child was having breakfast, his mom was feeding him with his favourite egg and mayo sandwich. The little champ kept turning around to have a look at me and was busy trying to understand my expressions. He could only see my eyes as I had my mask on.

In some time his mum realised that he wanted to have constant eye-to-eye contact with me, so gave up trying to feed him and turned his chair to face me.

I realised the child wanted to be friends with me and was persistently staring at me, completely expressionless. Then, I removed the mask from my face and smiled back. His face lit up, and he smiled too. He had a pair of dimples and we ended up sharing a smile constantly without feeling tired.

In Singapore it's unusual to see locals smiling back, so my day was brightened because of his smile, that had a mesmerising effect that stayed with me throughout the day.

I feel a stranger can become the best of friends when they share a heart-to-heart smile.

COEN

2am, 29 December 2014, Hamad International Airport, Doha.

It was in the early hours and I'd just taken a few hours flight from Barcelona, and was in transit home to Singapore. With eight hours between my flights, the aviation lounge full, and not wanting to spend two hundred bucks on a few hours-sleep in a hotel, I decided to rough it out in the complementary rest area. However, as a light sleeper, I couldn't sleep because the room was a symphony of snorers!

Just as I looked up, I saw a lady seated right across from me and I could see she was feeling very uncomfortable too. So, I did the natural thing, I smiled. She smiled back, and we began chatting.

What do two strangers chat about in a foreign airport?

Of course, we talked about the typical questions…

'Where are you from?'

'Where are you going?'

'Where were you travelling from?'

I found out that she was on the way home to Jakarta, having spent the past month in Istanbul with her Turkish boyfriend.

As we chatted, she suddenly started tearing up. She shared that she was feeling very sad, because she was in a long-distance relationship with her boyfriend. When she was in Istanbul, he was very loving to her and wanted to make love to her every day. However, when she was back in Indonesia, he would send her pictures of him being with other women, and say that they were more beautiful than her.

What a jerk…

It was inconceivable to me that such people exist. I listened and then asked why didn't she just leave him?

'I thought of it … But it's hard! I love him and he tells me that he loves me a lot and that he will take care of me. He was very sweet to me whenever I was with him.'

I'm usually not someone who would jump in with advice for other people, but I couldn't resist speaking up.

'Come on, you need to set boundaries to protect yourself. If you want the relationship to go somewhere, you've got to tell him how you feel about what he's doing. Otherwise, he's going to take you for granted. If he really loves you, then he will not be doing this kind of thing to hurt you. That's not love, that's emotional manipulation.'

I kept her company as she sobbed it out. After that, she smiled and said, 'Thank you! I feel so much better now being able to speak about it. You're right. I have to take care of myself first.'

The time just flew by. Instead of sleeping, we spent the time chatting, two strangers in transit in an airport rest area, forming a deep connection.

MASAMI

As I said in the introduction to this lovely book, I'm an introvert. Speaking to strangers is not something I do naturally, but I tend to get approached by strangers often. I'm usually the one that attracts all the salespeople and fundraisers on the street. Strangers tend to approach me asking for directions, even when I don't look like a local resident. I don't think I look so knowledgeable either. So, I've eventually figured the reason I get approached is because I tend to have a smile on my face most of the time. And I have experienced some life-altering moments because of this, too.

Numerous times, I was approached by people who were in crisis situations. Those who got robbed, or lost access to their life-saving medication. I marched into accident cases; I took people to police or to hospital.

I don't think that changed their lives - because if it wasn't me, someone else would've helped them. But at least, I could say those moments changed my life. It's a special honour and a gift when you get to help make a difference for someone else.

NATHAN

Assumption is the enemy of empathy. Often we assume that our leaders know they're valued, that those close to us know we love them, or that our colleagues realise we respect them. It's not always the case.

As a personal branding specialist, I have the privilege of working with leaders spanning a variety of industries, with positions of varying heights. The kinds of people who give a lot of themselves to their teams and those they lead, day in day out. Beyond their remuneration, they often receive very little by way of uplifting encouragement, connection and empathy. We assume they don't need it.

While travelling abroad with friends, we were exploring a mountain village when I received a text message that stopped me in my tracks. The words were unexpectedly revealing, kind, and heartfelt. For years I'd been encouraging a high-calibre leader, who had been under a lot of public pressure. Although I was unsure of how the words were being received, I sent them anyway.

That day, on the side of that mountain, I was reminded that pushing past assumptions toward empathy, matters.

A casual word of encouragement, in season, often means more than we assume.

The gestures that we deem as small, have the power to find their way through the hearts of people; regardless of whether it's a friend, a stranger, or someone we assume doesn't need it.

Together, let's resist making assumptions about who needs to be encouraged.

Offering someone the gift of a smile or an uplifting word, may just change the way they see the world, and their place in it.

KERRIE

I often forget how much my encouragement might mean to someone, or how it can build their confidence in some way. I hope that I've added a little light to someone's day, but I can't know if it means a little or a lot. So I give it anyway, when I see the opportunity to do so.

In September 2019, Lyndon and I arrived at our accommodation in Brisbane. I posted this on Facebook after a few minutes of pondering what felt like a profound conversation with our driver.

> I hugged our Uber Driver today.
> I'm pretty sure that's a first.
> He shared a few stories of passengers and I saw what a kind soul he is.
> I thanked him for the difference he makes in the small moments.
> #DoTalkToStrangers 😄🩶

I'd left my card with him in case he ever wanted to connect and tell me more stories about talking to strangers. So I shouldn't have been surprised when I saw that he found my profile online and commented on my post.

'Kerrie, what you don't know is how much I needed a hug today. That hug made a huge difference to my day. It was greatly appreciated and bought on a tear as I drove off. Then to see the above is one of the most flattering things to ever happen to me. Thank you for listening. This stranger is grateful.' ♥

I replied and acknowledged the powerful reminder that it matters when we DO Talk to Strangers.

A conversation under my post had begun. Colin continued the next morning…

'My parents taught me that the world needs a guy who changes strangers' flat tyres in car parks or pushes a broken down car across an intersection. The guy who picks up stray dogs bolting down a busy street after a thunderstorm or mows the elderly neighbours lawn. Many times in my life I have asked strangers in distress if they are okay, and as a result twice I have carried sick or elderly complete strangers to medical centres in my own arms. These actions have been a privilege not a chore. Importantly I don't think I am unique for it and I do not seek praise for it beyond what those people gave me at the time.

I have seen others do the same and I am sure if I were not there at those times someone else would have stepped up.

Yesterday didn't start so well for me. So the real story here is that your hug improved my day and then this post added to that. Thank you. You made my day. The world needs more people like you, not me.'

I felt a little uncomfortable with Colin's last comment and didn't want to include it. Yet in exploring my discomfort, I see the humanness - the relatability. Most of us can easily see how someone else is more kind, thoughtful, or compassionate. We can see the value in others more than ourselves. I disagreed with Colin's last comment, and I've kept it in here as it's a key point in this book. The world needs you, and your unique ways, and opportunities to support others. Your small acts of kindness, your moment of listening, expressing concern for someone is more important than you realise.

The simple act of paying attention can take you a long way. **Keanu Reeves**

COACHING CORNER

BEING HELPED

Can you remember a time you felt more confident or assured because of the support of another?

What courageous steps have you been inspired to take?

HELPING OTHERS

When did your genuine smile, greeting or support mean more than you thought it would?

What small offer of support or act of kindness can you do today?

Who can you encourage this week?

PART 3

Making a bigger difference
in the world

IMPACT

How has talking to a stranger had a positive impact far beyond what you could have imagined?

Our little moments of connection, our pauses to listen to someone, to really hear them, or the split-second decisions we make can have significant impact. These might show up in your own life, the life of another, or countless people around the globe. In many cases, you'll never know the impact you made way for, created or inspired.

When Steve Jobs shared his story, he said, 'You can't connect the dots looking forward; you can only connect them looking backward. So you have to trust that the dots will somehow connect in your future.'

This is really useful to remember that we don't know what's ahead, we don't know if we'll benefit from this or some other interaction - or if others will - and so we give without strings attached. Perhaps we've simply contributed to some dots connecting in another person's future. We are all interconnected whether we see it or not.

ANNA

Talking with strangers on a meaningful level broadens your world, challenges your assumptions, helps you connect the dots, stirs something in you, and inspires you with evolving ideas. And we end up feeling a whole lot less lonely and on the back foot in this crazy world of ours.

NATHAN

Talking to a stranger has the power to create a positive impact, an effect far beyond we could imagine.

Many of the stories in this book share a common thread. A very ordinary thread, that is somehow extraordinary at the same time. Without realising it, many of us have created an impact by doing something we think is very normal, like starting a conversation with the person sitting next to us.

Once we'd reached cruising altitude, on our journey from Tokyo to Sydney, I realised that this wasn't going to be just another ordinary flight. I could tell he wanted to share something. Something that weighed on him.

Over the next 9 hours, we chatted about business, discussed family and explored faith and theology. Ultimately, we landed on the matter that weighed heavy on his heart. As conversation unfolded, it became clear that by sharing the difficult experiences I've walked through in my own life, he was able to make a little more sense of the health trials his family was facing.

For one of us, it was just an open conversation. Yet for the other, it unlocked so much more.

Walking beyond the immigration point with luggage in hand, he explained what it meant to him, and how it changed the way he saw his situation. He touched down in Sydney, carrying less than he had taken-off with.

Most of us wonder if we have much to offer. You do. Could your story impact someone? Let's find out, by listening and then sharing, to create a positive impact far beyond what we could imagine.

LYNDON

I've discovered the power of listening and asking questions that do not have an agenda. While walking the Camino de Santiago, people said that walking with me and sharing their story gave them more clarity than their sessions with a therapist. Perhaps it was that they didn't have expectations of their time with me like they did with a therapist, but I saw that listening and accepting someone where they were at could make a powerful difference, especially when coupled with an agenda-less question. I distilled what they said to me and repeated it back to confirm I had heard them and could empathise. This increased their understanding of their own situation as they heard themselves think, and it seemed as if my paraphrase of their situation gave them a new perspective, or language to articulate that which was inaccessible to them due to their closeness to the situation.

Also, as we each shared our journey, we gained understanding or encouragement for our own lives. I don't know what many of them have gone on to do, or how they help others, but I'm glad I could help them in that moment. That is all we can do, really. Be ourselves, be there for others and accept them where they are at and expect that we may never see the good that has come from it, but trust it will.

JULIE

I spoke at an Administration Symposium for a health organisation here in Dunedin in 2017. That day I told my Why Not story, my response to going blind by replacing 'No' to opportunities that came my way with, 'why not?'

Six months later I was standing in our local bakery on a Saturday morning when I got a tap on the shoulder. 'Hello Julie, it's Judy from the Administration Symposium'; just the way I had taught them to introduce themselves. Then Judy continued, 'You changed my life that day you spoke, Julie.'

Touched by her words she told me of how she had been afraid of flying and her daughter - who lived on the north island of New Zealand - had always been asking her to go and visit the family. 'She asked me recently, and I just blurted out, 'WHY NOT!'' said Judy.

Wow! I felt humbled by her story and excited for her new growth in confidence, and all it had taken was me sharing my story.

KATIE

My husband Andy and I had a very fortuitous meeting with a young couple at the wedding of a mutual friend in the fall of 2017. They had just returned from several months of travelling abroad and were on such a high from their trips. We had only just met them, but their enthusiasm was so contagious! I started probing for more information about how they planned the trip, because I knew this was something we had to do.

A year-and-a-half after that meeting, we quit our jobs and set off on our own adventure. That meeting was absolutely life changing. If we hadn't had that conversation, I'm not sure we would have ever had the courage to really plan and make it happen, leaving it up to the all-too-common, 'Someday'. That conversation resulted in a lifetime of priceless experiences and memories.

UNAMI

Being an African person living in Australia, I know what it's like to be a foreigner a long way from home. Whenever I am in a public place and I see another African person, I make a point to acknowledge them through a smile or even introducing myself, depending on the context. When I was living in Port Hedland, Western Australia, I made connections with other African women and ended up with an incredible African sisterhood, most of whom were women who I met in public places such as grocery stores.

These women became my support persons, my confidants, my babysitters, my advisers and just sisters from another mother. For a lot of these women, we ended up being part of a group that met up every few weeks to eat together, pray together, laugh together and just do life together. The women went on to set up a not-for-profit to help support other people who were struggling financially overseas. It never occurred to me that being friendly and opening myself up to friendships would yield such golden moments and experiences that went far beyond a casual conversation. I owe that rich experience to the willingness to talk to strangers.

SERENE

I took a trainer certification course 13 years ago. In my class sat two individuals I'd never met before. I love talking to people, so we chatted. From this simple connection over the two-day course, I was introduced into the world of training.

One was the owner of a training provider, whose company grew enormously in the following decade. His company helped keep workers in their jobs through government subsidies, through difficult recessions, and shifts in market demand. I trained thousands over the next 12 years and was always proud of the fact that I helped people be economically active again after they'd fallen on hard times.

The other was a founding member of a non-profit organisation who worked on the issue of senior care - a national priority for Singapore, the country with the fastest ageing population in the world. We helped older persons to regain their independence, younger persons to rethink their ageist opinions, and organisations to rework their processes to be more age-friendly. To this day, I am happy to work with them in corporate and community training.

All of the work I've ever had from training can be traced to these two connections that I made one day in class with strangers who sat on my table, and were willing to give someone who had never trained a day in her life a chance.

ANUPAMA

One day, my husband urged me to go along with him to meet Rinchin, who had just moved to Singapore. He had been requested by an old mutual friend to meet up with her and give some advice. Reluctantly, thinking that I would waste two hours of my time on a busy day, I made him promise me a cappuccino date in return for the favour.

Little did I know that an important person was walking into my life.

As she and my husband chatted and I chipped in with some advice myself, I saw Rinchin's eyes light up every time I said something to her.

We then connected on social media and loved each other's social media posts and writings. That one coffee meet-up turned into weekly meet-ups, late-night movie dates, selfies, girly-heart-to-heart chats and escapades.

She did not know though that with each interaction with her, my excitement was growing. You see, for a few years, I had been feeling like I wanted to create something by combining my love for having meaningful conversations and relationships with people and also fanning the creative flames in myself. It was a dream book project - I wanted to create it with contributions from more than 100 inspiring people. Also, I wanted to do it with someone who would share my dreams and vision for this beautiful book, so that it became an enjoyable journey, to be remembered forever. I had been searching for many years for the right person to be my co-author.

After about a year of interacting with Rinchin I decided that she was just the right person for me to ask to partner with me and bring my dream book to life. One day, I told her I wanted to tell her about a project that I wanted her to do with me. And she said, 'YES!' without knowing what it was, trusting someone she had met just a year ago. This was pure serendipity.

This one connection that came to me from thousands of miles, and helped me bring my dream to life, makes me believe that we meet people for a purpose that we may not always immediately understand. Because, there is no other way to explain how a chance meeting that I got pulled into, helped us become such close friends, despite an age difference of 18 years, and create something amazing together.

Some of the contributors in the book have also now started to meet each other and collaborate. I hope to see many more strangers bond over our book, creating more meaningful connections, finding support both in their network and with strangers, to share their dreams, follow their heart and live more purposefully.

I am glad I said, 'Yes.' Like Kerrie says, 'DO Talk to Strangers!'

PATRICK

I worked as a business relationship coach for an attorney who was struggling to build her practice. She is a self-described introvert and dislikes attending networking events because she doesn't enjoy talking to strangers. She is very well connected in her area of expertise, and I suggested that strengthening her existing connections would be an effective way to achieve her growth objectives.

She took my advice to heart and a couple of times a month she would identify people in her network who would benefit from knowing one another. She would invite them out to lunch and facilitate what was inevitably an interesting conversation. Often, her invitees would discover similarities, or opportunities to help one another. Regardless of the degree of connection that her guests established, the attorney almost always received heartfelt phone calls, emails, and texts thanking her for arranging such an enjoyable experience. The goodwill that she generated from these lunches has been the most important factor in a dramatic increase in client loyalty and referrals.

The attorney's success in connecting her connections inspired me to start doing more of this myself. When I look at my first-degree connections on LinkedIn, there are hundreds of people I know who could benefit from meeting each other. While I enjoy making these connections in the real world, this isn't possible in this time of pandemic-induced 'social distancing'. Yet, with video conferencing, it's easy to invite two people to a 30-minute virtual coffee. I've made it fun using a green screen and the backdrop of a favorite coffee shop. I don't try to be the most interesting person in the virtual coffee shop. Rather, I simply want to be interested in asking questions of my guests so they get to know each other and see possible ways that they might be able to help each other. The positive feedback I receive from my connections after facilitating virtual meetings reminds me of the favorite business relationship building principle from my book, The Connector's Way, 'Serve others without consideration for how you will benefit'.

When you generously help others and lift them up, it will come back to you!

KALEY

The thought that immediately comes to mind was my unforgettable lunch with Michael, the CEO of a major finance company. I was really nervous when I arrived for our lunch. But I needn't have been, because Michael was so friendly and down to earth. He told me about his children and asked about mine.

Michael explained why it's important to be a good person. On your own, your prospects are limited; but with a team of supporters, you can achieve so much in life. The more kindness and humility we display, the more friends and allies we attract. Michael turned out to be right. All the successful people I met on my 100 lunches journey were kind and humble, just like Michael.

Michael didn't just teach me a valuable life lesson during that lunch; he's taught me many valuable lessons since. That's because Michael generously agreed to become my mentor.

How incredible - a star businessman taking me under his wing. So a random lunch with a stranger in 2018 turned out to be a life-changing event.

COEN

On the same cruise trip I mentioned previously, my first cruise as a speaker, I continued giving my series of speeches, often to crowds of just ten people or less.

After one of the speeches, a couple came up to me and spoke to me. 'Coen, we have been married for 30 years, but we feel we're about to come to the end of that! When we're back in Sydney, we're going straight to file for a divorce.'

I gulped…

'Well, it seems then, it's a rather curious choice for you to come on a cruise ship!'

'Yeah, this is the trip of a 'Last chance saloon' for us really. We wanted to give it the last chance to see if we can really stand being together. Can we find time to speak?'

'Well… Yeah, for sure, why not? We have plenty of time on the ship!'

So we spoke.

I had thought it could be a tricky conversation, and I certainly didn't want them to throw each other overboard!

To my surprise, it took all of forty-five minutes, listening to them, and asking questions. The issues had gone a long way back in time, but I was able to help them to identify clearly their motivations for their actions, what they had expected from each other but did not communicate, and their blind spots in understanding that had contributed to the situation exacerbating. I then gave them some suggestions and communication exercises to do during the trip, and how they could keep themselves in check when they're triggered.

On the final day before we arrived in Sydney, I bumped into them again. They came to me and said, 'Coen, we want to thank you so much, because you've saved our marriage! We have never been more in love with each other.'

So there I was, thinking that I was too young, and too inexperienced to speak about relationships. I would never have thought my enrichment lectures could alter the course of a couple's marriage.

Unknown to me, that was a profound moment of insight and permanent change to my psyche. Before that day, I always had 'authority issues' - I would shrink and feel smaller in the presence of people who have bigger titles, more economic success or more years on earth than me. I struggled and never knew how to find a way out. The refrain, 'believe in yourself ... love yourself', had never really worked for me. I knew it at a cognitive level, but not at an emotional and visceral level. But I understood that day, that everyone, regardless of titles, position and wealth are just human beings. We have basic human needs, and we're doing the best we can at every moment to fulfil them, though we often fall short and are figuring things out as we go along.

Today, people ask me, 'Do you feel intimidated when you're talking to big corporate companies? Do you feel inadequate when you're speaking to people more senior and experienced than you?'

My answer is, 'Yes! Of course! To feel that is human, and is a healthy sort of intimidation. It makes you step up and stretch yourself, then you'll realize you're actually stronger than you thought you were. And also then, I no longer see people for their titles, I see them as people.'

GANESH

In July 2017, scrolling through Linkedin, I was intrigued by Kerrie's profile featuring DO Talk to Strangers. I'd only ever talked to strangers when they had made an appointment to see me professionally or after sharing their details with me in advance.

After connecting with her online, and reading her book, following her adventures, and offering some advice for connecting with the media on her first trip to India, we met up in Singapore. We met with no barriers and we shared our stories and insights.

Since then we have expanded each other's networks, meeting up for many dinners over the past few years. In fact, this expanding network of inspiring individuals is how I came to know the Mayor of Mandello, Italy, as Kerrie had introduced me to Jessica Fabrizi, whose grandparents were from there and I decided to offer support as mentioned earlier.

This has been a transformational journey. I'm now confident and open to connecting with strangers everywhere I go, and grateful for the experiences.

I remembered my original reason for studying communication in the year 2003, which I shared with my interviewer at St Xavier's College Of Communications. Mr Sudarshan asked me why I chose to be in communications. I remember closing my eyes, reflecting for a few seconds and replying to him saying, 'God exists between me and the other person when we speak heart-to-heart'. He was taken aback by my impromptu reply.

We are transformed by our connections with others, inspiring or creating transformation in many more ways than we imagine.

MASAMI

Today, I run an organisation called B1G1, which is a giving initiative. We help businesses of all kinds to integrate effective giving in what they do so that they can create life-changing impacts just by doing what they do.

Some of our members have cafes, giving access to life-saving water for every coffee they serve, or accountants helping educate children in need for every great meeting they have.

Kerrie is one of the amazing business people I met through the work B1G1 does. Because we are here to 'create a world full of giving' we get to meet some of the most giving and caring people in the world.

I founded this organisation because I saw so many issues in the world during my travelling days. I deeply cared about how those issues were affecting the people I met and eventually became friends with. I didn't know what I could do back then, but I never forgot about the kindness people shared with me. In those days, I was often invited to the homes of families who didn't seem to have much food to feed their own children. But somehow, they were generous enough to share whatever they had with me - a stranger from a foreign country.

So, when I became a parent and had my own kids, I felt it was important for me to do something about some of the children in the world who didn't have the same kind of privileges my kids had.

With that, I started my first business nearly 20 years ago - a food company - because I believed that food connected people. I worked hard for years, trying to grow the business so I could **one day** give back and help feed and educate vulnerable children.

After years of hard work though, I realised how difficult it was to succeed in business - to the extent you can do something significant - like taking time off to dedicate to social work.

One day, the simple idea of B1G1 came to me, and it transformed my business perspective forever. I realised that it's better to do a small thing every day instead of trying to do a huge thing 'one day'. We decided to give a meal to a child in need by supporting an experienced organisation - for every meal we sold.

I also realised there were so many other entrepreneurs and business people who cared about our world, but they were also too busy doing what they were doing. Eventually, I sold the food business and moved to Singapore to start a global giving initiative, aiming to help businesses make a real difference in the world by coming together.

Today, B1G1 works with thousands of businesses around the globe. Those businesses have created more than 200 million giving impacts over the last decade. We have all kinds of carefully selected giving projects that make tangible impacts on the lives of people around the world. And B1G1 passes on 100% of the giving coming from businesses to those important causes.

The 200 million 'impacts' is not just a big number. Those numbers include hundreds of thousands of trees being planted and millions of days of access to life-saving resources and quality education for people and children globally.

These 'impacts' are enabled by small acts of kindness by so many small businesses and people who work in them. It's a real proof of the 'power of small'.

Thinking back, I realise the smiles and kindness I received in my travelling days led me to this work. And I'm so lucky to be doing what I do with some of the most amazing people in the world.

So ... I guess that's the power of talking to and connecting with strangers.

One day, I think you will look back and have a similar reflection. You'll realise how those connections you had with strangers transformed your life and lives of many others.

Enjoy the journey - it really is amazing!

CATHY

I've lived in Singapore for 22 years. On my first trip here, I had an experience with a stranger that resulted in a huge lesson for me about Singapore - and helped to lead to my decision to move here.

It was July 1998, my first trip to Singapore and to Asia, and through friends from Chicago, my partner and I were asked to join a couple for dinner one evening. My partner was working that day and planned to go to the couple's home from work, but I was asked to meet one of our hosts at her workplace and she would drive me to their home for dinner.

She sent me specific instructions - take a subway to the Aljuneid Station, exit the train, take the escalator down to a bank of payphones (yes, it was that long ago), call her and she'd come there to pick me up. My little subway trip was going well, and before long I was at the Aljuneid Station, standing in one of the long lines of people waiting to get to a pay phone.

My turn came, and I stepped up to the phone, but when I tried to find the coin slot, I realized it was a type of pay phone that only took a special kind of card - one which I didn't have. Disappointed, I turned to go to the back of another of the lines, one which led to a coin pay phone, when the young teenage boy behind me walked up, slid his card in the slot and said, 'Here, you can make your call.'

I was stunned. In the U.S. I could imagine a teenager saying something quite different from that, more like, 'Get to the back of the line, lady!' But here was this young guy being very sweet to a total stranger. I told him, 'No, it's ok - I'll just get into another line,' and he said again, 'No, go ahead - make your call.' I finally said, 'OK, but take my coin,' and handed it out to him. He said, 'No.' I asked him a second time to take my coin, but he still insisted that he wouldn't, and asked me again to make my call. Finally, I stepped up and made my call.

The kindness that young guy showed me touched me more than I'm sure he'll ever know. I saw a country where young men showed more caring and less macho posturing. It wasn't long before my partner and I made the decision to make Singapore our home. To this day, I still experience this same beautiful approach shown by all kinds of people here, and it confirms my decision to live here. It's a refreshingly supportive place to live - and my experience of it started with the actions of a young stranger at the Aljunied Station in Singapore...

KERRIE

In a conference with 10,000 other women, I found myself next to Viviane, an enthusiastic young woman from Brazil. We had a little chat and connected on Facebook to potentially stay in touch, possibly for the duration of the conference, or to reconnect at some time in the future. No strings attached.

Several years later I was in Sydney doing a Facebook Live video with a friend from the USA, and Viviane messaged with great excitement that we must meet up while I was there! She traveled an hour across Sydney the next morning. Over coffee, she told me how she was in a class where the lecturer held up a copy of DO Talk to Strangers, wholeheartedly endorsing the message! Viviane was thrilled and told him how we'd connected years earlier. Soon after, I had a phone call from him, and then Paula Mills, the founder of the college, Academy of Entrepreneurs, enthusiastically asking me to visit their campus and speak to the students. I've since presented in many of their Sydney classes, and online to students from over 65 countries.

Paula and I traveled to the Philippines together in 2019, expanding each other's networks, increasing the impact of the change-makers we'd worked with previously. It was unbelievably rewarding to share this journey with someone so passionate, effervescent and committed.

Paula took me to a Grameen office in Manila, where we trained managers in their microfinancing organisation, who train thousands of Filipinos to lift their families and communities out of poverty. I then took Paula to Gawad Kalinga's Enchanted Farm, known as the 'Silicon Valley of the Philippines' to meet the social entrepreneurs who are also making history in the most positive of ways.

We can't fully understand, or imagine, the ripple effects of my brief connection with Viviane in 2012, but we're all grateful to be a part of making a difference in the world. You never know the impact of your connections. Let's keep our hearts open and say yes to those moments of opportunity to connect with other open-hearted people.

Many of our ripple effects are small - but they all matter. You might not see yourself in front of an audience, but your simple acts of kindness, practical help or kind words or smiles can be the assurance someone needs to make a positive difference in their own world.

I met two young people outside Black Tambourine, one of our favourite cafes in Dubbo, looking for a bus to get to the edge of town. It wasn't far, so I offered to drive them. One was from Taiwan and one from Japan, and they apologised for their 'Bad English' which I said was significantly better than my Mandarin or Japanese, sharing the few words I knew in their languages, We also shared a few laughs about pronunciation, and the randomness of me saying 'helicopter' in Japanese.

Several days later I arrived at Black Tambourine for a coffee meeting, and the staff told me that a savoury muffin awaited me. The young people I helped had gone back there and asked, 'What's Kerrie's favourite thing here?'

Shortly after this lovely surprise, I discovered a message from one of them on Instagram.

21 Oct 2019

Thank you so much take us to home 😊 😊

We really appreciate that and looking forward to try that cafe 😊 🖤

You're so welcome!!!

And thank you for the muffins last week!
What a lovely surprise 😁

It's a small token of our appreciation, hope you will like it.

Cause I have never seen someone as kind as you.

So we'll keep kind and help someone who need hand.

I loved seeing these messages, especially the last line. It is a beautiful, simple example of a ripple effect. I've seen many moments like this in the past year as people have shared acts of kindness in the Kindness Pandemic group on Facebook and so many other pages online. When people are inspired and grateful, they make decisions like this - to keep an attitude of kindness, an awareness of others and a willingness to lend a hand.
Kindness is contagious, addictive, and rewarding.

COACHING CORNER

Do these stories remind you of some of your own moments of connection?

_____

_____

Reflect on momentary meetings, or friendships that developed...

_____

_____

How did you meet? What happened?

_____

_____

Can you think of times you connected other people to each other?

_____

_____

What happened, or is happening because of this new connection?

_____

_____

How have you been part of someone's ripple effect?

_____

_____

Reflecting and Taking Action

CONNECTING WITH AUTHENTICITY AND GENEROSITY

When we reflect on the beginnings of great things, we find encouragement as we see the value of small things. This is often celebrated in the B1G1 community - 'the power of small'. A small insight can become a powerful idea.

One of our members and friends, Mick Hase, inspired by the 17 UN Sustainable Development Goals, and driven to make a difference, envisaged an event with a series of 17-minute speeches, bringing people together, to explore various ways to take action towards achieving the goals.

Working from his home office in Tweed Heads, he reached out through introductions, making new connections and finding others open to collaboration.

Mick staged the first SEVENTEENx on the Gold Coast in May 2019. He found the best part of the event was the conversations after the speeches and panel sessions, hearing how audience members were inspired and turning that inspiration into action. SEVENTEENx went on tour to five capital cities in its first year, also becoming an inspiring podcast. All of these events were possible because of connections Mick made along the way.

Mick identified the key business lesson in these conversations: we may have the best product, but it's the connections that are the most valuable. It's no longer about, 'What am I going to do?' but, 'What can *we* create?'

What ideas come to mind as you read these stories and discuss them with others? Who can you connect with, and what could be possible as you ask, 'what can we create together?'

We're all inspired in different ways. I am inspired by many people, including those in this book, who use their words to speak life, hope and encouragement. People speak in smiles and music and art and service in ways that lift others up.

My point is: you make a bigger difference than you know. It's more important than ever that we take notice of the people around us with an intention of kindness - whatever that looks like.

When I first spoke to my dear friend, Masami, about this book, she told me that as an introvert she isn't really good at talking to strangers. However, she reflected that when out running each day, she tends to consciously smile at strangers as she passes by, and often that leads to her connecting with strangers. Her experience shows us that we don't have to feel like great conversationalists to light up someone's day. We can simply serve with the gifts we have. Masami hasn't allowed her introverted nature to inhibit her from working every day to improve the lives of millions of people.

Kaley began intentionally connecting with strangers for her personal development, with humility and gratitude, to learn, to be inspired. When you connect with no-strings-attached, ready to contribute to others and holding lightly to your expectations, you'll be amazed at the people who come into your life.

Zig Ziglar's well known quote can be thrown around without thinking, 'If you help enough people get what they want you'll get what you want.'

This is not about helping people *in order* to get what you want, but simply helping people. There's a ripple effect from our actions, but it seems to stem from the intention of our actions.

People know when you're approaching them with a hidden agenda. They feel it. People want authenticity. If you want to sell me something - I'm ok with that - if it's clear. No one likes to feel caught in a web of manipulation. Hidden small print can seem to be everywhere - so you can misunderstand, and expect there to be a catch in a simple act of kindness. The truth is that there are many simple acts of kindness going on around us every day, but they're not so obvious, and rarely show up in news cycles.

As you read Brett Culp's short story below, imagine yourself in the situation, as the frightened traveller or the calm person sitting

---

Brett Culp
11 March 2020 · 🌐
•••

Today I sat next to a tough looking guy who was on his first flight. When the plane lifted off, he started crying & moaning. He was so afraid.

I said, "It's OK. I'm here with you. You're not alone." But he didn't say a word.

Four hours later, as we were getting off the plane, he looked at me and said, "Thanks for doing that."

We can't fix each other. But we can be present. We can show up. We can be voices of kindness when things feel impossible.

Sometimes that doesn't feel like enough. But I believe it is.

👍❤️ You, Lyndon Phipps, Amanda Max Cass and 146 others   6 comments 10 shares

| ❤️ Love | 💬 Comment | ↪ Share | 🌑 ▾ |

---

next to him. Perhaps you can see it from both perspectives. Sometimes we're the one who needs a little reassurance, and many other times we can give it, in little ways that make a difference.

This book focuses on moments of connection that can lead to beautiful things. The more we begin our connections with others from a place of authenticity, the easier relationship building can be. We can carry so much guilt, shame and fear, which inhibits our relationship building. When we become aware of this, we can begin to let it go and open ourselves to others in safe and rewarding ways.

On Being Present

When you're worrying about anything in the future, such as, will the relationship turn into anything profitable, you're unable to be fully present. I encourage you to create time to simply be in the moment, as you may learn something new. You may find, in giving yourself breathing space from constantly thinking about your situation, that clarity comes from the most unlikely places. A brain at rest, after working on a puzzle, is a brain primed for insight. So, let go of the pressure to 'get it right' and see what occurs when you're fully present, holding expectations lightly.

When we are aware of our thinking, we notice when it's not useful, and can learn to redirect our thoughts. Dr. Jeffrey Schwartz, one of the world's leading experts in neuroplasticity, demonstrates how focused attention changes the brain, through his presentations and books, including, You Are Not Your Brain: The 4-Step Solution for Changing Bad Habits, Ending Unhealthy Thinking, and Taking Control of Your Life.

What gets your attention? What do you give your attention to? It will shape your decisions, often unconsciously. Since first hearing Dr. Schwartz speak in 2008, I've been captured by his simple, profound statement - 'Attention changes the brain'. I keep asking myself and my clients, 'so what are you paying attention to?' This has helped me to manage uncertainty, stay calm under pressure, and kept me out of dramas on social media and elsewhere. It's helped me choose my focus in all kinds of situations, and gravitate to people who are also focused on solutions, kindness, and making a positive difference in the world. Yes, I've repeatedly used a word here - one that's so important to - well, pay attention to.

The work of Dr. Schwartz and others in the fields of neuroscience, leadership and coaching has transformed me. People are often surprised to know that a family friend described me at 19 years of age, as 'the most negative person I know'. I'm now aware of when my brain is taking me down an unhealthy path, which enables me to redirect my attention to positivity and a solution-focus. It has been a joy over the past 17 years to support others in their transformation.

There is an enormous and ever-growing field of neuroscience that has influenced this book - it actually influences all aspects of life, and makes complex things make sense. Some concepts in these pages, which might seem new, are 'no secret' and can be found in many publications, from science journals to blogs and articles. If you wish to know more - which I encourage as it's so fascinating - follow the work of these leaders in the field, and discover their peers and their work also. Dr. Jeffrey Schwartz, Dr. Daniel Siegel, Dr. Matthew Lieberman, Dr. Jessica Payne,

Carol Dweck, Jamil Zaki, Dr. Caroline Leaf, Brené Brown and Shirzad Chamine. It's exciting to see their work becoming familiar in popular culture from books to movies, and I love sharing what I learn and discovering more.

I've recently partnered with Shirzad Chamine to bring his world-class Mental Fitness program to help entrepreneurs and creatives who have big dreams and sometimes small self-belief.

'This work is a synthesis of the latest breakthroughs in neuroscience, cognitive and positive psychology, and performance science. The research is the basis of Shirzad's New York Times bestselling book, Positive Intelligence, and Stanford lectures.' - www.positiveintelligence.com

The outcomes with my clients have truly been stunning, as we have explored and discovered better ways to connect, innovate, collaborate, and stay calm and thoughtful in the face of great uncertainty. And, it's completely changed the way Lyndon and I do life together. It's far more fun and collaborative!

My Gratitude

Countless people have been part of this book - those who know about it, and many more who don't. I've been touched by your ripple effects and I appreciate you all. I'm grateful for all the conversations at cafes, along walking tracks, at parkruns in Singapore, our hometown of Dubbo, and Townsville, Far North Queensland right down to Sale, Victoria. From fancy events to supermarkets and street corners, everywhere I've travelled - including virtual travels through online communities - I've been inspired by those I encounter.

Every writer who contributed stories has given all of us a gift, with unknown ripple effects. Please let them know what their words have meant to you, via their websites listed at the end. I'm grateful for their involvement, their patience with me and each other, as we all navigated 2020 through vastly diverse circumstances.

The editor for this book, Val Clark, who's a published author herself, has been a significant support in wrestling punctuation into place, tidying stories and asking insightful questions. We've laughed, grieved and stumbled forward through an extraordinarily challenging year and I'm so grateful to share this journey (and the occasional cheese platter) with her.

Over many years, conversations, questions, ideas and information have become layers of inspiration and challenge, pushing me to continue sharing this message of connection, kindness and contribution. Organisations of passionate difference-makers including Asia Professional Speakers Singapore, B1G1 and Speakers Institute have dramatically increased my opportunities to connect around the world, to keep learning, listening, growing and contributing.

I'm very grateful for my coaching and mentoring training with Results Coaching Systems since 2004, which was a significant turning point. RCS became The Neuroleadership Institute, and over the years I've had the opportunity to learn directly from many of the world's leading neuroscientists. This has deepened my understanding of the ancient wisdoms I've grown up with and helped me make more sense of the world in a richer, deeper way.

I've always loved this verse from the New Testament, 'Finally, brothers and sisters, whatever is true, whatever is noble, whatever is right, whatever is pure, whatever is lovely, whatever is admirable - if anything is excellent or praiseworthy - think about such things'. (Philippians 4:8)

When we see this through the lens of neuroplasticity, to 'think about such things' (pay attention) we are changing the landscape of our brain. While ever I'm writing what I'm grateful for - and you're reading and contemplating what's beautiful in your world too, we're doing good - for ourselves and others.

A is for Awareness

I've heard fearful stories of human connection gone wrong, and experienced it of course, as I'm sure you have, and of course we get it wrong too - it's all part of being human.

We get it right, too. People are awesome to other people - often unexpectedly.

Jamil Zaki shares in his book, The War For Kindness: Building Empathy in a Fractured World, 'Listening to a stranger tell an emotional story, we can describe how they feel with considerable accuracy. Glimpsing a face, we can intuit what a person enjoys and how much they can be trusted. Empathy's most important role, though, is to inspire kindness; our tendency to help each other, even at a cost to ourselves. Kindness can often feel like a luxury - the ultimate soft skill in a hard world.'

One of the key insights from his work is that empathy is not a fixed trait, and we can grow, nudging ourselves toward greater empathy. You'll be familiar with this idea if you've read Carol Dweck's book, Mindset, which discusses fixed or growth mIndset.

My hope is that through this book, my previous books, and others that raise our awareness, we nudge ourselves and each other toward more kindness, empathy and collaboration. When we operate on a purely subconscious, default mode, we set ourselves up for misunderstanding and hurt.

As I wrote in DO Talk to Strangers, A is for Awareness. Many of the questions posed in the Coaching Corners, are designed to do this - and to inspire action - Starting Small. What are the Small steps you can take this week? Today?

The ASKING Model wraps up with G for Gratitude - because gratitude is a powerful connector. There are many opportunities to say something like one of the following lines … if 'thank you' is too formal, simply say 'Thanks,' then add what you're specifically thankful for … pick one and try it today!

Thank you for your kindness.
Thank you for your patience.
Thank you for your compassion.
Thank you for your understanding.
Thank you for your empathy.
Thank you for your creativity.
Thank you for your thoughtfulness.
Thank you for listening.
Thank you for your honesty.
Thank you for your help.

I appreciate the way you showed kindness to...

I appreciate the way you took the time to...
I appreciate the way you waited...
I appreciate the way you made room for...

As my friend Avi Liran, founder of DeliveringDelight.com says 'What you appreciate, appreciates'! He wears his branded T-shirt that says 'Let's Delight!' on the front, and on the back, 'Work in progress' - which is fantastic to remember. We're all a work in progress, and when our focus is on appreciating others, delighting others, from work to home and in transit, we enrich our world.

Be Sincere...

Statements of gratitude and appreciation like these are only powerful connectors when you're being sincere. Connecting with strangers is an inside job before it's an external experience. This is why How To Talk To Strangers is more complex than a simple 1,2,3 step process. It takes a personal (inner) shift of focus. It means choosing to be present, sincere and grateful. If it is your earnest desire to nudge your world toward greater empathy, understanding this is important. Our desire leads to our soul searching and shift in mindset.

This book hopes to inspire you to connect with others in ways that make a positive difference. Let's explore! Where can you talk to strangers?

You know your world. How can you safely and positively talk to strangers? Are you online? What are the platforms you can use, or would like to learn to use?

Do you want to share a positive message? Do you mostly want to listen to others? I recommend both! Especially listening first. When you become a better reader, you become a better writer. When you listen well, you'll communicate your own ideas well, and in a more informed, empathetic manner.

So have a play - a curious exploration - in positive spaces such as kindness-related groups on Facebook and other sites. Use Facebook live or Instagram Live to share your thoughts and build community. If you'd prefer audio only, you might enjoy Clubhouse or Twitter Spaces.

Do you enjoy receiving hand-written letters? It might feel like a blast from the past and you might think the days of a letter in the mail are over, however the joy remains for those who receive them. And since we love igniting joy in others, if we send cheerful mail we feel good, too. If it's something you think you'd like to get involved in - start asking people you know for their postal address, or offer to write to strangers through a local organisation or if you're in Australia - Connected AU - www.connectedau.com.au.

Writing and posting cards or notes is something I've endeavoured to make a more frequent habit over the past few years, and Lyndon or I can often be found in the Dubbo Grove Local Post Office in the late afternoons getting our mail posted just before the trucks set off with the day's mail.

Who could you post something to? Of course, handwritten notes can be hand delivered, or secretly left to be discovered later. Perhaps a note for your barista, postie or bus driver?

Did you know of The Handwritten Letter Appreciation Society? It's amazing what you find online when you start searching for lovely things related to connection and kindness. And yes, it's easy to get lost in reading and sharing hours of inspiration - but so much more useful than some of the rabbit holes you could find yourself down.

Did you know of the Singapore Kindness Movement? After years of appreciating their cheerful reminders across Singapore, on buses, trains and billboards, I was honoured to present a Connect With Confidence workshop with the team there, and loved hearing their stories and ideas. And did you know there's a World Kindness Movement? The mission of the WKM is to inspire individuals towards greater kindness by connecting nations to create a kinder world. Did you know of Preemptive Love? There is a story of light in the midst of the darkest places, love and compassion, bringing down walls.

I could fill pages with names of organisations and individuals creating ripple effects, but as you explore, you'll find the ones that capture your imagination, and you'll find communities you connect with who cheer you as you create your own impacts.

I'd love to hear your ideas and stories of kindness, connection and positive ripple effects. If you're sharing on social media, you're welcome to tag me or any of the contributors who've inspired you. Or pop us a note in the mail!

Resources & Connecting

CONNECTING WITH OUR CONTRIBUTORS

Every contributor is a beautiful human being and making a difference in a variety of ways. I'm delighted to share their contact details so you can get to know them more. Please explore their pages and connect as they have so much to offer.

Anna Sheppard - www.bambuddhagroup.com
www.linkedin.com/in/annasheppard2021

Anupama Singal - www.anupamasingal.com
www.linkedin.com/in/anupamasingal

Coen Tan - www.coentan.com
www.linkedin.com/in/coentan

Cathy Johnson - www.linkedin.com/in/coachcathyjohnson

Conor O'Malley - www.conoromalley.com.au
www.linkedin.com/in/conoromalley

Ganesh Somwanshi - www.krescendocom.com
www.linkedin.com/in/ganeshsomwanshi

Julie Woods - www.thatblindwoman.co.nz
www.linkedin.com/in/thatblindwoman

Kaley Chu - www.kaleychu.com
www.linkedin.com/in/kaleychu

Katie Swanson - www.theswanderers.com
www.linkedin.com/in/katie-swanson-freelance

Kerrie Phipps - www.kerriephipps.com
www.linkedin.com/in/kerriephipps

Lyndon Phipps - www.atasteofawe.com
www.linkedin.com/in/lyndonphipps

Masami Sato - www.masamisato.com
www.linkedin.com/in/masamisato

Nathan Shooter - www.nathanshooter.com
www.linkedin.com/in/nathanshooter

Patrick Galvin - www.theconnectorsway.com
www.linkedin.com/in/patrickgalvin

Serene Seng - www.sereneseng.com
www.linkedin.com/in/sereneseng

Simon Jacobs - www.professionalweirdos.co.uk
www.linkedin.com/in/simonjjacobs/

Unami Magwenzi - www.firmo.com.au/

Related Reading

- The Connectors Way - Patrick Galvin

- The Trusted Way - Patrick Galvin

- 100 Lunches With Strangers - Kaley Chu

- Trust - Begins and ends with self - Conor O'Malley

- Mindset - Dr. Carol Dweck

- The War For Kindness: Building Empathy in a Fractured World - Dr. Jamil Zaki

- Social: Why Our Brains Are Wired to Connect - Dr. Matthew Lieberman

- You Are Not Your Brain: The 4-Step Solution for Changing Bad Habits, Ending Unhealthy Thinking, and Taking Control of Your Life - Dr. Jeffrey M. Schwartz

- Braving the Wilderness: The quest for true belonging and the courage to stand alone - Brené Brown

- Positive Intelligence: Why Only 20% of Teams and Individuals Achieve Their True Potential AND HOW YOU CAN ACHIEVE YOURS - Shirzad Charmine

Do you host a book club?

Get your tissues out - your members will share some moving stories of their own! Use the questions in the Coaching Corner sections to get the conversations started, and please reach out to us via www.kerriephipps.com for more resources to support your members.

A little more about B1G1

B1G1 is a giving initiative, making it easy for even the tiniest of businesses to make a positive impact in the world by creating a giving habit and tracking their growing impact long-term.

With this unique model, businesses can join the 'movement' and integrate all kinds of micro-giving in their everyday activities, knowing 100% of their giving is passed on to the causes they support.

Every purchase of this book also makes a difference as we give access to life-saving clean water to families in developing nations.

If you are a business owner, I hope you will choose to be part of B1G1. If you work for a company, you can recommend B1G1 to your company, too. If you do choose to join, please register at www.b1g1.com and use this special referral code **GIVING005** to receive a welcome Giving Credit from me and be linked to the growing community of caring 'strangers'.

Together, we really can change the world.

Connect With Kerrie

As a speaker and leadership coach, Kerrie inspires and equips audiences with thought-provoking and practical tools to develop the confidence they need to expand their network and create more opportunities.

Kerrie collaborates with you to make your event or team day a high-impact, meaningful experience, creating new connections, deepening learning and maximising opportunities for growth.

Sessions include

- Do Talk to Strangers - Connect with Confidence
- Increasing your Positive Intelligence & Mental Fitness
- Leadership Conversation Frameworks

Personal Leadership Coaching is a unique journey for each individual. When you're clear on the conversation in your own head, you can have authentic, confident conversations with everyone you interact with. The essence of our work together is increasing your clarity and confidence - with profound outcomes. You're asked timely, intuitive questions that deepen your awareness of who you are and how you connect with others. You'll build your mental fitness, and be empowered to step boldly into your aspirations.

Connect with us today to explore possibilities!

+61 409 982 342
www.kerriephipps.com
Sending mail? PO Box 172, Dubbo, NSW, Australia, 2830

More books from the author

DO Talk to Strangers - How to Connect With Anyone, Anywhere

Connecting with others is an essential ingredient for success in life and business. Meeting someone new could change the course of your life.

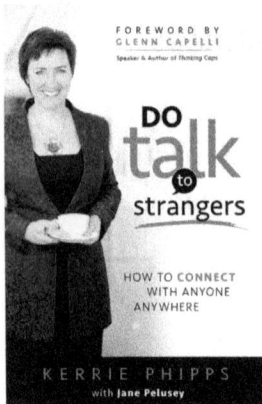

- Easily and naturally talk to strangers, including famous and influential people
- Use the simple ASKING model to connect with anyone, anywhere
- 5 Steps to Stunning Customer Service
- Wisdom for safe and insightful conversations

  'Do Talk to Strangers is a joy to read and a valuable resource.' - Glenn Capelli, author of Thinking Caps

Do Talk To Strangers - Travel Toolkit

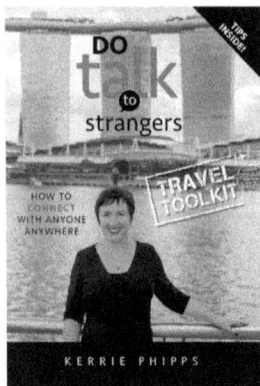

Travel with Kerrie through different countries and cultures, on a journey to seeing the world in a new way, through the lens of the unique ASKING Model.

'This book is a pleasure. It's sweet, short and full of lovely little tips. It's written in the same way that Kerrie greets the world; open-minded, excitable, a beaming smile and a can-do attitude.' - Lord Simon Jacobs

Lifting the Lid On Quiet Achievers - Success Stories of Regional Entrepreneurs

Lifting the Lid on Quiet Achievers is a practical, down-to-earth book that highlights entrepreneurialism and innovation in regional Australia, and shares specific tools and ideas that will immediately empower you.

'Whether you live in the country or city, this book will move you and your business to greater heights.' - Jenny Bailey, best selling author, former ABC Rural Reporter

Create the Life Journal - Journal Your Way To The Life You Want

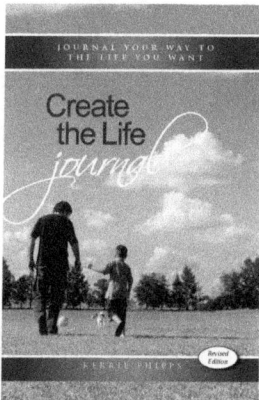

Clarity comes through writing, and clarity allows you to Create the Life You Want. Discover some amazing insights as you move through this journal, seeing the creative power of your words as you capture your best thoughts on paper.

'I was 19 years of age when I wrote down in a journal an audacious goal - to write and publish 16 best-selling books. Today, just 8 years on, I am proud to say I have achieved that goal. That is the power of writing down thoughts and flashes of inspiration. So go on, grab your copy of Create The Life Journal today!'
- Dale Beaumont, Creator of the Secrets Exposed Series

This book will be read by those who
know they're making a difference,
those who hope they have
(yes, you have, and more than you know)
and those who might have reached out in kindness
and been misunderstood,
and stepped back.

Please don't be silenced by
misunderstandings and judgments
of less-generous people.

Let your light shine.
Someone needs you.